The Killing

TV Milestones

THE KILLING

John Alberti

© 2017 by Wayne State University Press, Detroit, Michigan 48201. All rights reserved. No part of this book may be reproduced without formal permission. Manufactured in the United States of America.

ISBN 978–0-8143-4212-1 (paperback); ISBN 978–0-8143-4213-8 (ebook)
Library of Congress Cataloging Number: 2017934986

Wayne State University Press
Leonard N. Simons Building
4809 Woodward Avenue
Detroit, Michigan 48201–1309

Visit us online at wsupress.wayne.edu

CONTENTS

v

Introduction

The Killing *as Feminist Noir*

> The most important thing to me is not to
> pornographize murder. . . . I want to show
> the real cost . . . when a child is lost.
>
> —*Veena Sud, showrunner for*
> The Killing

> "We got the bad guy."
> "Really? Who's that?"
>
> —*Final conversation between detectives*
> *Stephen Holder and Sarah Linden at the*
> *conclusion of* The Killing, *season two*

Loved and loathed, left for dead and twice revived, few recent television series have provoked such intensely mixed reactions as did *The Killing*, Veena Sud's transposition of the Danish television series *Forbrydelsen* to Seattle (as played by Vancouver, B.C.), when it premiered on AMC in April 2011. Derided by some for its slow pacing and relentlessly dreary mise-en-scène, its supposed aesthetic inferiority to the Danish original, and especially the switcheroo in the first season finale that pushed the resolution of the murder mystery into season two, *The Killing* still managed to retain enough of a loyal fan base to make it through three seasons on AMC. Then, to the astonishment of many, *The Killing* was resuscitated yet again for a final six-episode series resolution on Netflix. Why, in spite of

An isolated Detective Sarah Linden gazing at the bleak and overcast skies of Seattle formed the iconic title image of *The Killing*.

flat ratings, was this show so hard to cancel? Why did *The Killing* inspire such obsessive fan behavior among both its fans and critics alike?[1]

One possible answer stems from how *The Killing* exemplifies a significant international gender revolution in one of the most enduring and tradition-bound American television genres, the police procedural. Along with other recent Anglo-American programs such as BBC's *The Fall*, the New Zealand auteur Jane Campion's *Top of the Lake*, TNT's *Rizzoli and Isles*, CBS's *Cold Case*, and drawing on earlier models such as *Cagney and Lacey*, *Prime Suspect*, and even *Veronica Mars*, *The Killing* features a female character in a role long coded not just as male but as representing the essence of what masculinity means: the lone wolf noir detective.[2] In focusing on a female character who is emotionally distant and guarded, who is wary of intimacy and the entanglements of domestic relationships, these new gender-switch procedurals clearly challenge dominant stereotypes of feminine identity. But this strategic casting reversal is not enough to explain why *The Killing* so excited and frustrated viewer expectations or why the program has achieved milestone status after only four seasons and forty-four episodes. Premiering at a historic crossroads in the rapidly evolving landscape of television in the digital age, as the basic cable revolution in creating "quality" original programming was spreading to "over-the-top" (OTT) online services like Netflix and Amazon, *The Killing* took advantage of the resulting opportunities created for generic and formal experimentation to translate global trends and influences, including the auteur-centric boutique model of the BBC and the brooding atmosphere of Scandinavian noir, into a feminist reimagining of the police procedural.

Throughout its four seasons, *The Killing* used and ultimately subverted the thematic and formal components of the classic androcentric noir tradition not just to switch gender roles but to use this upending of gender genres as part of a larger exploration of the pathology of masculine violence. *The Killing* turned the noir police procedural away from a focus on agency understood as personal autonomy and toward agency understood in terms of human relationships, especially in terms of the impact of violence on those relationships. From a relentless focus on and even obsession with finding the killer and thus "solving" the mystery, *The Killing* signaled a turn toward the consequences of violence, not whodunit but the damage done, not solving or resolving but dealing with the enduring trauma of violence.

It is this feminist revision of the noir narrative that results in the formal aspects of *The Killing*—its slow pacing, its extensive focus on the agony and agency of victims, and most of all its decentering of the drive to "solve the case" in favor of character and relationship development—that viewers found most irritating and most fascinating about the series. As Kristen Warner and Lisa Schmidt argue in their essay "Reconsidering *The Killing* as a Feminine Narrative Form," *The Killing* combines the differing generic expectations of the police procedural and the soap opera melodrama to create a tension between the linear drive of the murder mystery and the emotional intensity of melodrama, "a focus on the pathos of characters more than on the logic of police work."[3]

In making their argument, Warner and Schmidt draw on the ways that cinematic and televisual melodramas, especially in the form of the "women's picture" of Hollywood's Golden Age and the venerable soap opera, both daytime and prime-time versions, of radio and television, have been reclaimed and repositioned by feminist criticism. On the one hand, an emphasis on style and emotion over plot in the women's picture along with the open-ended resistance to final closure and resolution that defined the soap opera can work as critiques of dominant patriarchal narrative models. On the other hand, women and gender-conforming viewers of melodrama can find identification and empowerment in the foregrounding of issues—family relationships, sexual politics and violence, the forced primacy of the domestic in women's lives—that have been regarded as trivial or marginal by mainstream, usually male, critics and historians.[4] And as we will discuss further in chapter 1, the melodramatic has also functioned as a crucial subtext of the androcentric noir police procedural, however repressed or denied, as in the feminist literary critic Nina Baym's reference to the traditional male-centered classics of American literature as "melodramas of beset manhood," an apt description for the stories of lone wolf male detectives as well.

Unlike traditional noir and the classic televisual police procedural, from *Dragnet* to *CSI*, where the masculine hero uses violence as a substitute for the social connections and personal relationships he sees threatening his autonomy and agency, *The Killing* defines agency precisely in terms of relationships, and specifically the drive to protect and sustain relationships. For the hard-boiled homicide detective Sarah Linden, agency is inescapable from the relationships that give that agency efficacy and meaning. Though she is a supposed lone wolf, her life is defined and dominated by her relationships, including those with her surrogate mother/social worker, Regi; her son,

Jack; her partner Stephen Holder; and most of all the families blown apart by crime that we encounter over the four seasons of *The Killing*. These relationships do not stand in opposition to Linden's agency; their maintenance represents the whole point of having agency.

The threat that violence and trauma pose to human relationships informs Sud's mission statement for *The Killing*: "I want to show the real cost . . . when a child is lost." One helpful way to approach Sud's goal is to contrast the philosophical and existentialist trauma suffered by the classic noir male antihero with the material violence at the heart of *The Killing*. This violence includes not only the brutal murder of Rosie Larsen in seasons one and two, of the homeless street kids in season three, and of the wealthy Stansbury family in season four but also the use of violence as a means of restoring or asserting masculine agency, a classic trope of the traditional police procedural. Whether in the case of Rosie's working-class father, Stan, who over and over tries to fulfill this older, atavistic version of masculine agency in avenging his daughter's death, or the serial killer—and Sarah's former lover and police partner—James Skinner in season three, whose desire to protect the sanctity of his family results in his campaign to eliminate the homeless female teens he sees as a threat to his fantasy of domestic harmony, *The Killing* contrasts this culturally central idea of redemptive violence with a focus on the havoc created by violence.

Sud underlined her interest in the material reality of violence when discussing the challenges of adapting her Danish source text to an American context:

> We live in a society that is incredibly violent, much more so than Denmark [the setting of *Forbrydelsen*]. Amber Alerts are the norm, it seems, so much so, that a missing child, a missing teenager in a major American city, never makes the news. So the biggest challenge is to make us, as Americans, care about this young girl over a long period of time.[5]

Sud foregrounds the ethical imperative involved in the police procedural—how to "make us, as Americans, care about this young girl over a long period of time" (and not just until the mystery is solved)—into a focus on the interrelationships of the social that defines *The Killing* as feminist. In this way, *The Killing* as popular crime show can be accused of wanting to have its revisionist cake and eat it too, drawing in fans of the procedural with generically mainstream stories of murdered young women while simultaneously exposing the pathology of this generic formula. The degree to which viewers responded to this strategy as a bold feminist subversion of the police procedural or as a bad-faith version of it also accounts for the polarized reactions to the program.

Sud's strategy raises the questions that often went begging in complaints about the narrative competence of *The Killing*: Why exactly do we want to know "whodunit"? What is the narrative closure we desire in *The Killing*, or in any police procedural? Throughout its three narrative arcs and four seasons, the feminist noir melodrama of *The Killing* offered a circular rather than linear narrative drive, one that constantly revolved around the catastrophe indicated by the series' title, one that can never be "solved" in terms of repairing the damage done. The second season's implication of Rosie's aunt in the murder further frustrated the linear desire for revenge and closure and underlined the impossibility of closure, an impossibility that implies not just the ultimate futility of Linden's investigation but the futility of the very idea of narrative closure itself. Violence in *The Killing* is never an external force invading the sanctity of the family; violence is an intrinsic element of American society, of interpersonal relationships in a gender-imbalanced world. The "bad guys" are never safely out there in *The Killing*, and no detective or prison can protect "us" from "them."

In its third season, *The Killing* extended this critique of the police procedural to take on the even more starkly gendered conventions of the serial killer narrative. Rather than making the evil genius of the serial killer the center of the narrative, however, the season foregrounded mothers and mothering as a source of conflict and tension. When the killer turned out to be both outside and inside Linden's family of relationships—her ex-partner and lover on the police force—Linden herself turned both cop and killer, executing the "bad guy" and thus becoming one of two secret murderers at the heart of the season four mystery arc.

Its final six-episode season, made available for immediate binge-viewing on Netflix (another indication of how the series developed and reflected digital-age revolutions in distribution and viewership), *The Killing* focused completely on intrafamily violence, linking the abuse and cruelty concealed by the affluence of the murdered Stansbury family with the brutal world of a military academy, where sadism hides behind a veneer of chivalry, honor, and class privilege. A mix of gothic melodrama and noir thriller, the final season of *The Killing* connects Sarah Linden and the troubled teen Kyle Stansbury as detective and suspect, surrogate mother and son, and finally co-conspirators, each desperate to conceal and deny the violence that lies within the dysfunctionality of personal relationships. The "bad guy" turns out to be the face in the mirror, as both Sarah and Kyle must confess and atone for their own acts of violence.

Rather than referring to closure, Sud instead described the final episode of *The Killing* in more fragile terms. "From the very beginning, I knew that her journey would have to end in a place of uneasy peace, where there were no good guys, there were no bad guys. There was a truce that she had to make with the world as it is versus the way she wanted the world to be."[6] In the intensity of season four, designed to be watched in multihour viewing jags, *The Killing* fully embraced and merged the police procedural and the soap opera, noir and melodrama, confirming its faults to its critics and building on the intense emotional connections that fans of the show felt for Linden and Holder. True to form, the series ended with ambiguity, not about "whodunit" but "who cares whodunit."

7

After Linden discovers to her horror that, like her, Kyle is both victim and killer, and after her own violent crime is buried by the Seattle mayor who was her nemesis in seasons one and two, the series shifts ahead five years. Both Linden and Holder are off the force. Linden has been rootless, traveling the country; Holder has been working as a drug addiction counselor. They reunite, only to have Linden tell Holder she is leaving Seattle forever. At the end, however, he convinces her to stay. The ending can be read as a conventional romantic resolution, yet the exact nature of the intimacy between the two characters is never precisely defined beyond "best friends." Rather than affirming the cultural model of the lone wolf, *The Killing* affirms the necessity and moral centrality of human relationships, of relationships as the moral ground and justification for personal agency, not its negation. The series began with the Larsen family blown apart by tragedy and Linden's own frail network of personal connections breaking down; in the end, Linden finds at least the possibility of both partner and place.

The Killing appeared at a time in television history when experiments in gender inversion and subversion of traditional genres began to proliferate in a media landscape defined by multiple niche audiences and multiple viewing platforms, from *Broad City*'s feminist take on the bromance/gross-out comedy to *Orphan Black*'s pioneering feminist science fiction to *Orange Is the New Black*'s redefinition of the prison drama. Along with Gillian Anderson's portrayal of Stella Gibson in *The Fall* and Elizabeth Moss as Robin in *Top of the Lake*, Sarah Linden represents a crucial evolutionary moment in the specific history of the hard-boiled female detective in the television police procedural. These characters represent a critical intervention into the police procedural that rethinks the reactionary, isolationist tendencies of the genre in favor of a focus on community and relationships that represents male violence not (or not just) as a battle of wills between killer and detective but in terms of the impact of that violence on the families and personal relationships of the victims. The mix of fascination, bafflement, and at times resentment generated by *The Killing* reveals how radical this revision is for the future of the television whodunit.

The first chapter, "The Lonely Wolf: Sarah Linden and the Evolution of the Woman Detective," places *The Killing* in the history of the noir police procedural, from its origins in both cinema and literature through the development of the television crime show, in order to explore the difference gender plays in the formation of the classic lone wolf noir detective. The "lone wolf/lonely wolf" contrast provides a larger conceptual framework for tracing the genealogy of Sarah Linden within the more specific history of women detectives in televisual police procedurals, particularly the way the marketing of "alternative" detectives stigmatized these characters as both hypersexualized and not sexualized enough. The recent wave of neo-noir women detectives has developed in critical relation to the *Cagney and Lacey* binary, pitting the "normality" of the working mom in a stable marriage against the pathology of the single and isolated career woman. In the character of Sarah Linden, *The Killing* pushes back against this simple and simplistic opposition, as Linden both values and remains suspicious of traditional gender roles and family relationships.

Chapter 2, "Remade in America: Revising *Forbrydelsen*," looks specifically at how *The Killing* revises the original Danish series *Forbrydelsen* in terms of Sud's mission statement for the American version not to "pornographize" murder and to show "the real cost . . . when a child is lost." While the central marketing strategies of both series centered on having women play the traditionally male-gendered role of the gruff, no-nonsense, lone wolf detective, both series' initial storylines also emphasized Sud's idea of the "real cost" of murder through an extensive focus on the emotional trauma of the Larsen families caused by the murder of their daughters. They differ, however, in terms of the extent to which *Forbrydelsen* "pornographizes" murder by emphasizing the victim's sexual activity and making

9

her murder a brutal sex crime. Sud, instead, extended the murder investigation into season two, in part to further explore the emotional damage done to the Larsen family, all the while de-emphasizing the idea of Rosie's murder as a sex crime, both countergenre moves that alienated part of the American viewing audience. Even as *The Killing* tackled the serial killer trope in season three, a plotline conventionally associated with sex crimes, the narrative focused on the serial killer in terms of the structural pathologies of family and community, the killer a "bad father" obsessed with the threat of female sexuality. Rather than a "thriller," as *Forbrydelsen* advertised itself, *The Killing* instead followed the "feminine narrative form" of melodrama as suggested by Warner and Schmidt to create a procedural focused less on a linear obsession with "solving" crimes than on repairing the damage done.

10

Chapter 3, "The 'Real Cost' of Murder: Family and Relationships in *The Killing*," traces the evolution of privileging the consequences of violence through each season of *The Killing*. While season one most closely follows the narrative structure of *Forbrydelsen*, the subsequent seasons and storylines act as a mashup of the Danish thriller, using component parts from the three cycles of *Forbrydelsen* to at first invoke and then upend the conventions of the noir procedural, all in the service of creating a radically feminist revision of the TV cop show. In Sud's words, *The Killing* operates as an "anti-cop cop show," one that resists formal closure and the desire for a "solution." Instead, *The Killing* offers a critique of a fragmented American society that makes connections—family connections, political connections, social connections—impossible. In particular, in honoring the consequences of violence on the families involved, *The Killing* makes the parent-child (especially mother-child) bond a central symptom and bellwether of "who cares who done it." It's a bond that includes both literal parents and children but also extends to the idea of society as family, with how well we do or don't care for children the true measure of crime and violence. Rather than cynicism, however, in the end *The Killing* insists on that "uneasy truce" described above that allows for hope and the possibility of recuperation.

The final chapter, "From Cable to the Web: *The Killing* as Cult TV in the Digital Age," discusses the broadcast and distribution history of *The Killing*, particularly its resurrection on the OTT streaming service of Netflix after its cancellation by AMC, as an example of cult TV and binge-watching in the evolving digital era, as well as how the present era has coincided with a flourishing of feminist reconstructions of various television genres. The appearance of *The Killing* at a critical time in the rapid evolution of television in the digital age—the move from cable to web-based, OTT programming—turned what was most problematic about the series from a traditional marketing point of view—its tendency to polarize audience reactions—into a potential strength. AMC's decisions to renew the series after its controversial first two seasons and to drop it after season three point to the ongoing negotiation broadcasters and distributors have faced in the digital era between the traditional desire to create the broadest audience possible for a program and the powerful loyalty generated by the smaller but often demographically attractive niche viewers. Web-based, OTT programming has built on this niche-viewing trend to create a moment when the intensity of viewer interaction has replaced traditional ratings as a measure of business success. From this perspective, *The Killing* represents a case study in terms of the evolution of the business model for commercial television, its cult status a defining characteristic of OTT programming.

This destabilizing of the television business model and traditional models of television viewership have coincided with and facilitated a move toward feminist television represented by shows like *The Killing* and other contemporary women-centered police procedurals. As binge-watching moves from the fringes to a normalized mode of television viewership, historically conventional ideas of what is meant by a "TV series" or even an "episode" face potentially revolutionary changes. In resistance to the linearity of the police procedural, *The Killing*, a series defined by Sud's commitment to "slow-burn storytelling," anticipated the binge-watching model of OTT services.[7] As a landmark example of a radically new form of police procedural, *The Killing* stands as a bridge to further experimentation and genre revision.

The Lonely Wolf

Sarah Linden and the Evolution of the Woman Detective

> But the great pleasure of writing *The Killing* is to get to take all the tropes and clichés and formulas and either riff off of them or throw them out the window. That is the mindset I've had from the very beginning.
>
> —*Veena Sud*

13

*T*he Killing premiered on AMC on Sunday, April 3, 2011, bringing together several important trends in contemporary U.S. television. For the basic cable channel AMC, which began life as the American Movie Channel in 1984, specializing in airing movies from Hollywood's Golden Age, *The Killing* was the latest example of its aggressive move into original programming. Beginning with the iconic *Mad Men* and continuing with other landmark twenty-first-century programs such as *Breaking Bad* and *The Walking Dead*, AMC presented a challenge to HBO, Showtime, and other premium channels by developing their own auteurist television programming, provocative and formally innovative narratives marked and marketed by

Veena Sud.

their identification with distinctive creators and showrunners like Matthew Weiner and Vince Gilligan. In keeping with this strategy, *The Killing* is very much Veena Sud's show, and subsequent praise and criticism of *The Killing* were inseparable from evaluations of Sud as the program's driving force.

Born in Canada and raised in Cincinnati, Ohio, Sud started her career after graduating from Barnard College as an activist journalist, first with the progressive *Pacifica Radio* and then with the media watchdog group Fairness and Accuracy in Reporting (FAIR) before enrolling in the graduate filmmaking program at New York University.[1] She then worked with the producer and writer Meredith Stiehm on the CBS police procedural *Cold Case* (2003–10), a show that follows a female homicide detective named Lilly Rush (played by Kathryn Morris) who is charged with investigating "cold cases" no longer of active interest to the police; hence, the program's title and organizing concept. Sud credits her experience on *Cold Case* with *The Killing*'s foregrounding of the "real cost" of murder as its thematic and moral focal point: "[One] of the great similarities between *Cold Case* and this show [is] the unrelenting focus on the victim, where the victim is not just a prop in the cop story."[2]

The Killing also followed in the tradition of American remakes/revisions of successful international programming, in this case, the 2007 Danish self-described "thriller" *Forbrydelsen*, translated as *The Killing* (although "The Crime" is a more literal translation) when it was shown in a subtitled version on BBC Four in 2011. While the transatlantic adaptation of successful European shows is nothing new in the history of American television, as represented most famously by *All in the Family*, Norman Lear's take on the 1960s British BBC sitcom *'Till Death Do Us Part*, most pre-Internet examples of this practice assumed and even relied on the ignorance of U.S. viewers about the overseas originals. *The Killing*, on the other hand, as with other digital-age conversions like *Broadchurch* (UK)/*Gracepoint* (US) and *The Bridge*, hoped to capitalize on the buzz created by *Forbrydelsen*'s popularity in the UK as well as on the vogue for Scandinavian noir in literature, movies, and television, from Stieg Larsson's *The Girl with the Dragon Tattoo* trilogy to Henning Mankell's *Wallander* series.

Forbrydelsen also represents another important trend in Scandinavian noir that has the strongest implications for the milestone status of *The Killing*: "femikrimi," or mysteries and police procedurals centered on strong female leads. In adapting *Forbrydelsen* to an American context in *The Killing*, the most faithful translation centers on the main characters of Copenhagen detective inspector Sarah Lund, played by Sofie Gråbøl, and Seattle detective Sarah Linden, played by Mireille Enos. Both are single mothers, and both begin their series contemplating a career move based on their involvement in serious romantic

Sofie Gråbøl as Detective Inspector Sarah Lund, wearing her trademark sweater and jeans, in the Danish series *Forbrydelsen*.

relationships with men. Both characters are deliberately deglamorized, *The Killing*'s Sarah Linden retaining the bulky pullover sweaters that became the visual trademark of *Forbrydelsen*'s Sarah Lund. Each character performs the classic noir detective persona of the emotionally guarded loner, blunt in their interactions with their colleagues and uncomfortable with introspection and personal intimacy.

Both programs also share a distinctive visual aesthetic, a translation of the high-contrast light and shadow of classic film noir into a bluish-gray, desaturated, low-contrast mise-en-scène. Both Copenhagen and Seattle appear as gloomy port cities, with *Forbrydelsen* augmenting the sunless climate with the austere

An almost constant rain defines the oppressive atmosphere of The Killing, as does the claustrophobic confines of the unmarked car where the main characters, Detectives Sarah Linden and Stephen Holder, spend much of their time.

modernist architecture of Danish government buildings. For fans of *The Killing*, relentless, endless rain defines the world of Linden and Holder, the two main characters constantly rushing through downpours, each literally weighed down by their sodden sweaters (Linden) and rain-soaked hoodies (Holder).

That the presence of a strong female lead marks *The Killing* as both distinctive and part of an established subgenre of television crime program, just as the idea of the Scandinavian "femi-krimi" suggests both an anomaly and a trend, defined the particular cultural moment in the gendered evolution of the police procedural in which the show premiered. In both *Forbrydelsen* and *The Killing*, gender identity is both central to the characters of Sarah Lund and Sarah Linden and also no big deal, at least in an overt, thematically foregrounded way. That both detectives are women does not make them unusual in the eyes of their (mostly) male colleagues; *how* they perform gender does. This distinction is crucial to what is most innovative about *The Killing* within American television history and to the specific ways that Sud adapts her main character in terms of her larger goal of creating a procedural that does not "pornographize murder."

The Police Procedural

The history of the American televisual police procedural usually begins with the translation of *Dragnet* from radio to television in 1951. Focused on the professional, psychological, and sociological dynamics of policing as a form of organized work, the police procedural differs from the classic private detective mystery genre specifically in this focus on the social, on the institutionalized dimension of police work and crime solving. The private eye, on the other hand, the default mode for the character type of the lone wolf noir detective, deliberately operates on the fringes of and in many cases in opposition to "official" police work. When the lone wolf is placed within the constraints of bureaucratized police practice, his role as social rebel is accentuated, as in the *Dirty Harry* and *Lethal Weapon* movie franchises. This "plays by his own rules" character has by now become a cliché and source of easy parody within the noir procedural.

In this respect, *Dragnet*, the foundational police procedural on television, introduced a more complex version of the lone wolf police detective in Jack Webb's defining portrayal of Sergeant Joe Friday. A character who seemed completely isolated from all forms of social interaction save police work—unlike his partners, for Joe Friday over the two decades of *Dragnet's* presence on television there was no evidence of a "personal life" outside of the LAPD—his almost robotic, by-the-book lack of emotional affect signaled both his isolation from his coworkers and his embodiment of systematic, institutionalized procedure. Far from "playing by his own rules," Friday *was* the rules, his personal identity subsumed into his functional role within the LAPD machinery.

It is this tension within the police procedural between the personal and the institutional, the relation between individual identity and social ideology, that makes the police procedural a particularly resonant genre for studying the evolution of gender performance and meaning on television. Based in a working environment gendered even more exclusively as male than other occupations with which television has been obsessed over the years, from lawyers to doctors, the police procedural is also centrally positioned within matrices of race, ethnicity, and class in terms of its focus on crime, aberrance, and social order. Simply put, stories focused on law and order force us to think about just what we mean by "law" and "order," including the laws of gender identity and performance.

Police Procedurals and the Anomalous Woman

Beginning in the 1960s, contemporary crime thrillers and police procedurals began to compete with and eventually supplant the Western on prime-time network television. Many Westerns can, of course, be seen as versions of police procedurals, as in the archetypal mainstay *Gunsmoke*. Self-contained crime mysteries perfectly fit the short-story-like demands of hourlong episodic television, whether the crimes were taking place in the 1860s or the 1960s. The cultural turmoil of the 1960s, however, began affecting these traditional genres, both Westerns and crime dramas, and network television began a hesitant and self-conscious exploration of issues surrounding race, class, and gender, trying to find a commercially viable middle ground between intriguing and alienating what they saw as their core viewing audiences.

In 1968 ABC TV aired *The Mod Squad*, a high-concept procedural aimed at appealing to a young audience within the formal constraints of the televisual crime thriller, featuring three young members of the "counterculture" chosen/coerced to serve as a police undercover unit. The characters were carefully selected to achieve a fragile balance between stereotype and relevance: Pete (Michael Cole), a dropout in rebellion against his wealthy white family; Linc (Clarence Williams III), a young black man from Watts; and Julie (Peggy Lipton), a "flower child" who fled an abusive home life. Beyond *The Mod Squad*'s flirtation with the allure and exoticism of 1960s youth counterculture, Lipton's character of Julie was also part of a beginning experimentation with women in the roles of detectives and crime solvers, a recognition, however nervous and fitful, of the growing significance of the second wave women's movement.

The Mod Squad followed by two years ABC's first such experiment in gender countercasting, *Honey West*. The first American television series starring a female private eye, *Honey West* featured a title character (played by Anne Francis) influenced by the "Bond girls" in the wildly successful James Bond movie franchise, as well as the British television series *The Avengers*. *The Avengers* featured an international crime-fighting duo consisting of the character of Dr. Cathy Gale and later Mrs. Emma Peel and the dapper John Steed (Patrick Macnee). Gale was originally played by Honor Blackman, who left the series for the role of Pussy Galore in *Goldfinger* (Guy Hamilton, 1964), further cementing the connection between *The Avengers* and James Bond, and Peel was played by Diana Rigg when the show began airing on American television in 1966. The characters of both Honey West and Emma Peel embodied a contradiction perhaps inevitable in early experiments with gender in mainstream police procedurals: they were both assertive and sexualized, physically battling criminals while wearing form-fitting catsuits that confused their competence as crime fighters with their objectification as objects of sexual desire, just as the updated femme fatale "Bond girls" functioned as both sexual partners and worthy antagonists for Bond.

In a larger context, both West and Peel represent a specific stage in the evolution of gender roles in popular entertainment: the image of the "anomalous woman." The anomalous woman refers to a kind of containment strategy for stories featuring women in jobs and social positions normally coded as masculine. The women in these stories, like Katherine Hepburn's

Anne Francis as Honey West, a female action hero that embodied the contradictions of the anomalous woman in 1960s TV.

globetrotting journalist in *Woman of the Year* (George Stevens, 1942) or Polly Bergen as the first woman president in *Flowers for My President* (Curtis Bernhardt, 1964), potentially threaten the established gender order before finally assuming their "rightful" place—Hepburn's character as a supportive wife, Bergen's resigning the presidency after becoming pregnant. In short, the women in these stories are treated as anomalies, and their gender is foregrounded as the defining feature of their dramatic significance.[3]

In this respect, *Decoy*, an almost forgotten syndicated police procedural from 1957 heavily influenced by *Dragnet* and featuring a female NYPD detective, illuminates the changing representations of and reactions to the concept of the anomalous woman from either side of the cultural disruptions of the 1960s and 1970s. Shot in stark black and white on location in New York, *Decoy* starred Beverly Garland as the androgynously named detective Casey Jones. The title of the program referred to the recurring plot device of Jones going undercover,

Although her appearance conformed to 1950s constructions of femininity, Detective Casey Jones (Beverly Garland) in the early police procedural *Decoy* behaved more like the by-the-book cops in *Dragnet*.

a trope that continued throughout the later television history of women in police procedurals. In the case of *Decoy*, however, while the plainclothes detective Jones appears regularly in the "uniform" of conventional 1950s womanhood—dresses and skirts, a modest but definitely feminine hairstyle, full but tasteful makeup—she is never overly glamorized or hyperbolically sexualized. The acting on the program echoes the stoic, all-business style of *Dragnet*, and Jones's male colleagues rarely comment on the anomaly of her gender. Like Joe Friday, Jones appears to have no personal life outside her job.

Yet for all the matter-of-factness with which Jones is treated by her fellow officers, the premise of *Decoy* still depends on the novelty of her position. That *Decoy* exhibits less overt referencing of or anxiety over Jones's gender than later versions of the woman detective certainly is derived in part from the tonal influence of *Dragnet*, but the apparent acceptance of Jones on the police force also owes something to the pains the show takes to reinforce the enduring persistence of stabilized gender differences in the 1950s. Each episode of *Decoy*, for example, dedicates itself to the "Bureau of Policewomen" in the NYPD, reassuring viewers that the anomalous and potentially disruptive presence of women on the police force is carefully contained and regulated within a segregated "bureau," a civilian version of the "women's auxiliary" units established in the American military during World War II, from WAVES to WACS to the WAF.

The increasing visibility and growing influence of the women's rights movements in the 1960s and 1970s, however, undermined this containment strategy. The result was characters like Honey West and Mrs. Peel, who would use martial arts skills to fight and defeat men in physical combat, suggesting a breakdown of gender hierarchies that was countered by subjecting these characters to relentless sexualization meant to reinforce increasingly fragile gender boundaries. This increasing instability in the anomalous woman on the force is reflected in the title of *Police Woman* (1974–78), starring Angie Dickinson as Sergeant "Pepper" Anderson. A spin-off from the procedural anthology series *Police Story*, *Police Woman* differed from the single-season *Honey West* by achieving a mass audience and lasting for four seasons on NBC. Like Honey West and unlike Casey Jones, Dickinson's character is glamorized and sexualized; like both Casey Jones and Julie on *The Mod Squad*, her anomalous gender makes her best suited for undercover work. Unlike Jones, these undercover operations disproportionately centered on roles that not coincidentally created opportunities for Dickinson to appear in a variety of exotic fashions and states of semi-undress.[4] This basic premise was repeated in *Get Christy Love!* (1974), combining race with gender, as Teresa Graves starred as a black police woman who likewise worked undercover to capitalize on her dual "alternative" identities.

Cagney and Lacey (1982–88) marks a decisive breakthrough in the way female characters functioned in televisual police procedurals and prepared the ground for Sarah Linden in *The Killing*. Created by Barbara Avedon and Barbara Corday, *Cagney and Lacey* was a self-consciously feminist rewriting of

The 1970s series *Police Woman*, like *The Mod Squad* and *Charlie's Angels*, constantly created plot devices that required star Angie Dickinson to appear in sexualized and revealing clothing.

the "buddy narrative" in the police procedural. From one perspective, *Cagney and Lacey* continued in the tradition of the anomalous woman. The series was marketed on the basis of the gender identity of the two leads, and Tyne Daly's Lacey and Sharon Gless's Cagney likewise represented competing stereotypes of women's identity, the former a working-class mother and wife, the second a glamorized but lonely single woman.

Yet Cagney and Lacey were not relegated to special "undercover" assignments; they mainly worked as regular homicide detectives, and like Casey Jones their presence in the squad room was not treated as on ongoing source of anxiety and crisis. The ethos was instead that the idea of women on the police force was becoming normalized, not in the sense of transcending gender bias or sexism but as an unstoppable social development not relegating women to the separate sphere of the women's auxiliary.[5]

Cagney and Lacey, featuring Sharon Gless as Detective Christine Cagney (left) and Tyne Daly as Detective Mary Beth Lacey (right), represented a consciously feminist attempt to revise the depiction of women in law enforcement

Melissa Leo's character of Kay Howard on *Homicide: Life on the Street* (1993–99) followed in this same line as part of a police procedural more rooted in the dark noir tradition than *Cagney and Lacey*.

Still, the larger cultural binary that defined *Cagney and Lacey*—the choice between a traditional heterosexual marriage with children and the glamorous but driven "career woman"— persisted through the 1990s into the twenty-first century. While the number of procedurals featuring women in lead roles has increased to the point that the fact of a female character is no longer viewed as a shocking anomaly, they still reflect the tension represented by the anomalous woman in taking Cagney's single career woman and increasing her glamorization and sexualization. Kate Beckett in *Castle* (2009–16), for example, a show that combined the procedural, the private eye mystery, and the romantic comedy, is a former fashion model turned ace homicide detective. As Veena Sud described the trend, "In cop dramas, there's a preponderance of female cops who wear stilettos, and it drives me nuts."[6]

The Lone Wolf versus the Lonely Wolf

It is in the context of simultaneous progress and containment, of police procedurals featuring women characters in major roles but still glamorizing and (hetero)sexualizing them, that the international trend of noir-inflected police procedurals that challenge this model of the anomalous woman began to appear, starting with Helen Mirren's portrayal of Jane Tennison in the British series *Prime Suspect* in 1991 and culminating in *Forbrydelsen*, *Top of the Lake*, and *The Killing*. As Sud's comment implies, one of the self-declared goals of these shows is more realism in the portrayal of women in police procedurals: "'It was like, let's take every cliché of female detectives and ground them in reality, right down to their shoes.'"[7] Sofie Gråbøl, the star of *Forbrydelsen*, echoes this sentiment in reference to the pullover sweaters that became the trademark of both Sarah Lund and Sarah Linden:

> She and the film-makers knew that they wanted to avoid the cliché of the woman in a suit in a man's world, but they didn't know what to avoid it with. "Then I saw the sweater and I knew," says Gråbøl. "Because to me it is so on the spot. It tells so many things to me about the character, which meant I didn't have to act them. It tells of a woman who has so much confidence in herself that she doesn't have to use her sex to get what she wants. She's herself."[8]

The fact that Sud can refer to "every cliché of female detectives" proves how prevalent the role had become in the police procedural; that the role is already defined by clichés—stiletto heels, "the woman in a suit in a man's world"—demonstrates the endurance of the anomalous woman model of exploitation and containment.

Of course, the appeal to "reality" is problematic in its own way, although it is in keeping with the dominant ideology of the police procedural, which has always claimed realism as its defining ideal, most baldly in *Dragnet's* iconic opening voice-over: "The story you're about to see is true." Similarly, long-running procedurals such as Dick Wolf's sprawling *Law and Order* franchise (which combines the police procedural and courtroom drama genres) bank on a "ripped from the headlines" approach to maintain relevance and viewer interest, modeling storylines on current social controversies.

But the demands of genre and narrative convention greatly complicate the appeal to realism. *The Killing* remains a noir procedural, which means it draws on and necessarily revises the tradition of the construction of noir detective narratives and the formation of noir gender roles. And the word "noir" itself indicates a particular *perspective* on reality—world-weary, cynical, romantic, and disillusioned at the same time—rather than "realism." It's fairer, in fact, to talk about the innovativeness of *The Killing* in terms of how it challenges and rewrites the central formal and ideological logic of the procedural narrative, creating a model of noir feminist police procedural that pushes back against the binary model of the anomalous woman procedural. It is the radicalness of Sud's approach in *The Killing* that likewise defines its crucial revisions and alterations of the Danish original.

As I discuss in the introduction, noir is a crucial if initially surprising choice for this feminist revision of the police procedural. While the noir tradition can be read as reinforcing strict binary gender roles, pitting a hypermasculine lone wolf detective against various hypersexualized "femme fatales," its simultaneous deconstruction of the mathematical linearity of classic detective fiction undermines the central project of the murder

27

mystery: restoring order after the trauma of crime. Noir's willingness to skirt with and even pass over into parody can expose the lone wolf pose as just that—a pose, a performance, an unstable artifice meant to protect the lone wolf against a radically destabilized and even meaningless universe. Cases are less solved in noir stories than they either simply unravel or become moot with the deaths of the main characters. In this way, noir mirrors melodrama as subversive genres featuring frustrated closure, non-teleological and digressive narrative lines, and a focus on the personalities and emotional lives of the main characters over plot resolution. World-weariness and cynicism are emotions, after all, even if they are conventionally coded as examples of masculine stoicism.

What intrigued Sud about *Forbrydelsen* was specifically its noir-influenced slow and even meandering pace, what she referred to as "slow-burn storytelling."[9] While American fans of *The Killing* were upset when Rosie Larsen's murder was still unsolved after thirteen episodes, the first season of *Forbrydelsen* took twenty episodes to resolve the murder of Nanna Birk Larsen. Sud connected this resistance to the linear drive of the conventional procedural with her desire for greater authenticity: "'It's worth it to really look at the reality and the true price of a child's murder,' she said. 'If people want to wrap it up, they can watch one of the hundreds of other shows out there that wrap it up in an hour.'"[10]

In response to media criticism of the lack of resolution to season one of *The Killing*, however, she offered a rationale that more fundamentally challenges the ideology of the conventional procedural:

> Sud suggests that those who object to the show's red herrings (like the finale's last-minute revelations that a crucial bit of evidence may be fake, a good guy a bad guy and the bad guy actually innocent) may be looking for an old-fashioned procedural, which *The Killing* emphatically and radically isn't. "They're complaining that there are too

many red herrings?" Sud says. "Well, there's two ways to look at it. Either it's a left brain journey where you're just connecting the dots of who the suspects are or it's more of a holistic journey where a young girl is murdered these are the potential suspects and this is why."[11]

Here Sud draws on the most subversive aspect of both melo-dramatic and noir narratives—their resistance to linearity and "connecting the dots"—to fundamentally shift the focus of her police procedural away from solving the crime and toward "the reality and the true price of a child's murder." This more "holis-tic" goal is really a kind of anti-goal, in that the emotional tenor of *The Killing*, as well as other emerging feminist noir proce-durals such as *Top of the Lake*, recognized that there is no final reckoning of the "true price" of Rosie Larsen's murder (or any of the murders on subsequent seasons of *The Killing*).[12]

This ultimately unsolvable and unresolvable goal defines detective Sarah Linden's obsession in *The Killing*, and it's her de-sire not just to find the bad guy but to create a safe world for the young and vulnerable that defines the lonely wolf. The classic noir narrative emphasizes the futility of closure as well, offering instead, in the case, for example, of Raymond Chandler's *The Big Sleep*, a kind of cool nihilism, as when the classic lone wolf detective Phillip Marlowe observes in the novel's final pages, "What does it matter where you lay once you were dead. . . . You just slept the big sleep, not caring about the nastiness of how you died or where you fell,"[13] the classic noir version of "who cares whodunit." But we can read this nihilism as the functional equivalent in narrative terms of the "solved" mystery in that the absolute absence of meaning provides the same certainty as its plenitude. If Sud's adaptation of *The Killing* provokes viewers, it does so by directly engaging with the question of "what does it matter whodunit" in terms of a broader, relationship-based un-derstanding of agency, a reconstruction of the gender politics of the hard-boiled detective in relational terms.

From this perspective, solutions are always disappointments because they ask the wrong question—whodunit—instead of making us care about a young girl in a world where masculine agency is defined through violence and destruction. Caring becomes a kind of pathos of character that challenges the desire for epistemological certainty characterizing the whodunit. "We got the bad guy," Holder half-heartedly tries to reassure Linden—and, by extension, the viewers focused on finding Rosie Larsen's killer—at the end of season two as she is about to quit the force. "Really?" she replies. "Who's that?"

Linden's tone here may reflect the noir-inflected world-weariness of a classic lone wolf like Phillip Marlowe, but her only semi-rhetorical question is really a rebuke and rejoinder to Marlowe's "what does it matter where you lay once you were dead." For Linden, who began *The Killing* by doggedly refusing to give up on finding where Rosie Larsen's body lay, the location matters very much, not just to the crime-solving logistics of the police procedural but in terms of how Rosie was not merely an isolated victim but part of a web of personal relationships. To push back against the lupine analogy of the noir lone wolf detective, the lonely wolf recognizes the pack nature of wolf society, that for all her wariness about her own personal relationships and social institutions skewed toward the rich, male, and powerful, Linden maintains a fierce loyalty to the idea of the pack. In a key revision of the ending of *Forbrydelsen I*, season two of *The Killing* ends not with the Larsen family forever blown apart but with the surviving members gathered together to watch the poignant good-bye video that Rosie left them before she started on what she thought was going to be a grand adventure to see the world.

In the end, the most radical intervention made by *The Killing* has to do with this challenge to the fundamental structure and politics of the classic police procedural. Not content with simply diversifying the casting of the police procedural by featuring women in lead roles, *The Killing* marks a crucial turning point in rethinking the ideology of the genre's form. By focusing her critique of the classic procedural on the question of the "pornographizing" of murder, Sud places *The Killing*'s challenge to the lack of "realistic" portrayals of the female police detective within a larger framework of the gender politics of the noir-inflected police procedural. In a similar discussion of Jane Campion's *Top of the Lake*, which premiered between seasons two and three of *The Killing*, Emily Nussbaum marks this same difference in relation to David Lynch's influential and experimental procedural noir *Twin Peaks*:

> Speaking of corrupt institutions, "Top of the Lake," which ends up revolving—like "Twin Peaks" before it—around sexual exploitation, suggests alternatives to television's typical approach to the subject, which too often relies on hot bruised corpses served as visual candy.[14]

There are bruised corpses of young women in the first three seasons of *The Killing*, but like *Top of the Lake* the series refuses to pornographize them. Instead, the final vision we see of Rosie Larsen in *The Killing* is one created by the character herself, and again in a significant change from *Forbrydelsen*, it is a character not primarily motivated by a romantic relationship but instead by a desire for personal autonomy and expression, for finding a meaningful place in the world. It is the disruption of this journey through violence that becomes the central wound in *The Killing*, and this particular revising and revisioning of the murder of Nanna Birk Larsen also marks how *The Killing* does not just adapt but recasts the gender politics of the Danish original *Forbrydelsen* in ways that produced the love/hate reaction that *The Killing* engendered. In the next chapter, we will examine how this focus on the restoration of family and resistance to the lone wolf model demonstrates how *The Killing* created a more radical challenge to the police procedural than did its Danish predecessor.

Remade in America

Revising Forbrydelsen

A dark, rainy, ominous night. A terrified young woman flees through the woods, stumbling over roots and bushes, apparently in fear for her life from a pursuer. While she remains the focal point of the handheld camera work, her face is hard to see in the underlit scene. The glare of a flashlight signals the presence and increasing proximity of her pursuer, whose identity is equally obscured. The scene ends with the young woman pinned against a tree, mouth opened in a scream as the flashlight blinds the viewer.

Both *The Killing* and *Forbrydelsen*, its Danish inspiration, open with almost identical versions of this scene, which we quickly learn shows the main victim, Rosie Larsen/Nanna Birk Larsen, shortly before her violent death. While both series then proceed to another similar scene of the main character's police colleagues staging a going-away party for her, the transitions between these scenes reveal some key differences between the two series, differences that go to the heart of *The Killing*'s revision of the Danish original and its landmark status as an American police procedural.

In *Forbrydelsen*, a shock cut connects Nanna's scream to detective Sarah Lund (Sofie Gråbøl) being jolted awake in her bed at home, as if she had been dreaming of Nanna in peril or had some other kind of psychic connection with her. As she rises, we see she is not alone in bed, and she walks away from the camera in only a shirt and underwear, a sexualizing shot that continues when her fiancé awakens to join and comfort her, and they begin to kiss. *The Killing* begins, however, actually before we see Rosie fleeing through the dark woods. In a scene visually linking the victim and the detective, we first encounter Sarah Linden (Mireille Enos) on her morning run through the woods, clad head-to-toe in an androgynous cold weather jogging outfit and hooded jacket, both sky and land the desaturated gray-blue that defines the visual motif of the series. The camera initially pursues her from behind, a visual cue made more ominous as we intercut with the scenes of Rosie running for her life through the woods (presumably) the night before.

The crosscutting continues the identification between Linden and Rosie. When the point of view switches to a head-on view of Linden, we then switch to a head-on view of Rosie running to the camera. As we switch back again to a side view of Linden, the crosscut now connects her with Rosie's pursuer. Finally, as Rosie falls face first on the ground toward the camera, also at ground level, the shot of the doomed Rosie filling the screen cuts to a black object on a beach that Linden arrives at in the background. With the music (also drawn from *Forbrydelsen*) building suspense, Linden approaches what looks suspiciously like a body. Moving seaweed aside, we see it is some kind of dead animal washed ashore, a discovery both disturbing and suggestive of the transformation of the murder victim into an anonymous object.

33

Linden is then interrupted by a phone call that leads to what she believes is a murder at a dockside warehouse, where she is told to enter the shabby, dilapidated building and locate the crime scene on her own. In a scene reminiscent of the tele-visual noir of *The X-Files*, she explores the murky interior with a single flashlight beam, spotlighting smears of blood before locating what appears to be a body draped in plastic and hung from the ceiling. She pulls away the plastic to reveal a blow-up sex doll; the "crime" is really an elaborate ruse and surprise party set up by her fellow detectives. After her bedroom scene, Sarah Lund in *Forbrydelsen* also attends a similar party, but hers is located in the brightly lit squad room. While the blow-up doll is also there, the scene lacks the menace of the opening of *The Killing*.

The Killing's revisions of the opening of *Forbrydelsen* could simply be chalked up to the American show's desire to add some individualizing touches to the process of adaptation, but these touches take on added significance in the light of show-runner Veena Sud's stated desire to show the "real cost" of mur-der and especially her goal of not wanting to pornographize the death of the teenage female victim. On the one hand, in both series the main character is a female detective who, in the tradi-tion of Jane Tennison from *Prime Suspect* and even Dana Scully from *The X-Files*, defies gender norms in order to better fit the model of the classic noir lone wolf: emotionally withdrawn and inexpressive; blunt and even rude in her interactions with col-leagues; mothers who seem to lack any semblance of maternal instinct.

Yet *Forbrydelsen*'s opening first "normalizes" Sarah Lund and softens her potential gender nonconformity by emphasiz-ing both her partnership in a heterosexual relationship and her heterosexual desirability. While *Forbrydelsen* can be read as setting up its viewers by appealing to their own conventional genre expectations regarding the smart but "hot" female detec-tive before undermining those expectations through Lund's

Mireille Enos as Detective Sarah Linden.

later difficulties in maintaining a pretense of gender norma-tivity, *The Killing* crucially introduces Sarah Linden to us nei-ther in her underwear nor in any kind of relationship. Lund's thick sweaters became a ready signifier of how deglamorized her character was, but her American counterpart even more completely rejects the trappings of conventional screen femi-ninity, eschewing makeup, her hair unstyled and gathered into a functional ponytail. It is not until episode four, "A Soundless Echo," that we see Linden in an erotic scene with her fiancé, at which point the isolation of her character and her suspi-cion of intimacy have already been well established. Instead, she is isolated when we meet her, a lone wolf running through the woods, and her subsequent search of the warehouse both creates immediate suspense and underlines her identity as detective, not woman-as-detective.

From its opening title credits, *Forbrydelsen* emphasizes its generic identification as "A Thriller." The tension between these two poles of our emotional investment in the police procedural—a vicarious and even illicit "thrill" in participating, if only voyeuristically, in the transgressive violation and murder of a young woman as part of the socially sanctioned effort to "solve" the crime versus an empathetic connection to the almost unbearable grief and trauma caused by that murder (the "real cost" Sud alludes to)—defines *The Killing* as a feminist revision of the police procedural, a revision that challenges the idea of "the thriller" in terms of both the form of the genre and its cultural meaning and purpose.

While most American reviews and discussions of *The Killing* acknowledge the existence of its Danish original/inspiration, few offer any substantive comparative analysis of the two; this is due in large part to the difficulty in the United States of accessing the English-dubbed version of *Forbrydelsen* that was a hit on the BBC. While favorable reviews and essays about *Forbrydelsen* have appeared in U.S. media,[1] most articles on *The Killing* rely on Sud for information about *Forbrydelsen*. But a more detailed understanding of exactly how *The Killing* remakes *Forbrydelsen* in America not only sheds light on specific plot developments that have been the cause of critical debate over *The Killing* but provides a case study in what are the most fundamental and significant revisions Sud and her production team made to the televisual police procedural in general and the evolving subgenre of the female noir detective in particular. In this chapter, I will highlight how Sud and her main team of writers play off of *Forbrydelsen*, building on the foundation of the lone wolf female detective and especially the emphasis on the damage done to the Larsen family. Retaining the slow, atmospheric pacing and gray exteriors of the Danish original, *The Killing* rearranges and redefines plot elements from *Forbrydelsen* to subvert the classic formula of the police procedural, in the process subverting viewer expectations in ways that fans found both compelling and frustrating.

Coming to America

In transposing the main crime of *Forbrydelsen*—the brutal murder of a young woman—from Denmark to Seattle, Washington, Sud was aware of the vastly different social contexts involved. In discussing his intentions for *Forbrydelsen*, the show's creator, Søren Sveistrup, wanted his story of a violent killing and political corruption to shake the complacency of Danish society: "'I think we sometimes have to look in the mirror and think, We're not always cozy, we're not always Hans Christian Andersen . . . Lego, Tivoli—that's our P.R., that's how we lure you to come here, but we're just as corrupt and power-sick as everyone else.'"[2]

The Danish society depicted in *Forbrydelsen* is much more centralized than that of the United States. Copenhagen is the cultural and political center of the country, and the series is the product of the Danish public broadcasting network DR, which dominates Danish programming. The municipal and later federal political machinations that form one of the two intertwined plots in *Forbrydelsen* take for granted the existence of an extensive welfare state supported even by conservative politicians. In this context, the murder of Nanna Birk Larsen is framed as a shocking anomaly to the supposed rationality and civility of Danish society.

The U.S. context is, to say the least, different, as we saw in chapter 1 when Sud emphasized what she saw as the "clear societal difference between America and Denmark," the fact that American society is "incredibly violent, much more so than Denmark." In *Forbrydelsen*, the death of Nanna Birk Larsen grips the national media, as does the race for mayor of Copenhagen. Sud faced the challenge, regardless of her larger intentions for

The Killing, of how to make Rosie Larsen's murder more than just another blip on the local Seattle news and, in terms of episodic television, more than just another example of an attractive young victim serving as fodder for the police procedural.

In adapting the dual storyline nature of *Forbrydelsen*, which juxtaposed the murder investigation with a hotly contested race for mayor, *The Killing* had to deal with the intense regionalism of the U.S. context—a race for Seattle mayor would barely register in other parts of the country—and the taken-for-granted nature of American violence that Sud alluded to. The more competitive American media environment brought additional pressures. Where the experimental nature of the Danish original—its non-gender-conventional hero, its noir atmosphere and slow pacing—was counterbalanced by its appearance on the main network viewing option for Danish viewers, *The Killing* developed in the current hypercompetitive era of television viewing in the United States, where it became one of dozens of crime shows available through cable, satellite, and Internet viewing.

The massive proliferation of scripted television series over the last ten years has divided the viewing audience into ever more specialized and self-selecting niche subgroups. At the same time, AMC, like other new content providers challenging the dominance of broadcast networks, is always searching for a hit among the niches, a series that either gathers prestige and critical attention (like *Mad Men*) or becomes so popular that it actually rivals the viewership numbers of broadcast TV (like *The Walking Dead*). As we will explore in greater detail in chapter 4, while *The Killing* benefited from AMC's willingness to support experimentation in form and style in order to create a niche series of distinction, its survival was always in question. That the program was renewed for a second season the week before the season one finale underlines the risks involved in further deferring the "solution" of the mystery past the end of the first season, and its subsequent cancellation/resurrection before season three and migration to Netflix for season four highlight *The Killing*'s daring in the face of its tenuous existence, again a dramatic contrast with the relative stability enjoyed by the creators of *Forbrydelsen.*

Over the course of its four seasons, *The Killing* engaged in a mix-and-match of narrative and thematic elements from *Forbrydelsen.* While seasons one and two follow the general overall story arc of *Forbrydelsen I*, the subsequent seasons build on the distinctive identity established by Sud's transformation of setting and purpose in those first two seasons to develop storylines strikingly different from those of *Forbrydelsen II* and *III.* At the same time, the course of *The Killing* can also be viewed as a mash-up of the Danish original, with component parts of all three seasons of *Forbrydelsen* abstracted and recombined in ways that provide narrative ingenuity but more importantly work as part of *The Killing*'s feminist revision of the noir procedural. While *Forbrydelsen* followed the pattern of inserting a gender-nonconforming noir detective into the generic formula of the police procedural, *The Killing* plays off of and often frustrates that formula in ways that expose the gender politics of those structural elements.

39

Revising *Forbrydelsen*

> I kept the foundation of the original format, which I loved—one episode is one day in the life of the investigation, and the three worlds colliding: the family, the cops, the political world. But what I had to do was infuse each [story] with a specifically American tone and sensibility.
>
> —*Veena Sud*

Before going into a season-by-season analysis of how *The Killing* challenges the lone wolf paradigm of the conventional police procedural (chapter 3), we can summarize the main ways that *The Killing* borrows from and revises *Forbrydelsen.*

Sarah Linden vs. Sarah Lund: Undoing the Logic of the Anomalous Woman

As the description of the two opening sequences above suggests, *Forbrydelsen* takes pains to underline Sarah Lund's normality and heterosexuality right from the beginning. She is identified as lover and wife first, then a homicide detective. In keeping with Søren Sveistrup's reference to the perceived order and rationality of Danish society, Lund operates as an anomalous woman, one who doesn't quite fit into what is otherwise a functional social order. That *Forbrydelsen* offers a noir-inflected corrective to the complacency of the Danish status quo does not change the fact that Lund is sexualized right from the beginning, so that part of her anomalousness derives from confusion that such a potentially attractive woman "hides" her beauty behind her unglamorized wardrobe.

Conversely, *The Killing*'s Sarah Linden is introduced more in the tradition of a lone wolf male detective, isolated from others and not immediately embedded in a stabilizing domestic role. Her character is tight-lipped, defensive, uncomfortable around people, and difficult to work with. That Linden is also a mother and involved in a romantic relationship that is leading her to leave the police force is only revealed after we see her "on the job," even if that initial job turns out to be an elaborate hoax. In both her romantic and maternal roles, however, Linden's gender role nonconformity continually accentuates her temperamental unsuitability for either role conventionally understood. In a broader context, again in keeping with Veena Sud's evocation of the more violent and less socially cohesive context of American society, Linden's inability to "fit in" is linked to a more radical view of the dysfunctionality of the social contract in the United States. Sarah Lund in *Forbrydelsen* is apparently the product of a conventional Danish family, as signaled through her stereotypically prickly relationship with her conventional mother, who constantly criticizes Lund's child-rearing lapses and urges her to marry and settle down.

Unlike Sarah Lund in *Forbrydelsen*, Sarah Linden in *The Killing* has no secure family life and is effectively homeless as she struggles to raise her son, Jack.

Sarah Linden, on the other hand, was given up by her mother as a child and spent her formative years bouncing from foster home to foster home. In the first season, we meet her surrogate mother, Regi Darnell (Annie Corley), her former caseworker who took Linden under her wing. Rather than singling out Linden as a "bad mother" the way Lund is in *Forbrydelsen*, *The Killing* places Linden's maternal failures in the larger context of how the social structure makes "mothering" of all kinds almost impossible. Throughout the four seasons of *The Killing*, mothering is thematized and radically problematized, beginning with the killing of Rosie Larsen over the course of the first two seasons; a season two plot twist focuses on the trauma of Rosie's mother, Mitch. Season three features Linden's relationship and eventual bonding with fellow "bad mother" Danette Leeds, and season four focuses entirely on intrafamily violence.

Challenging the Convention of the Sex Crime

One of the main attractions of *Forbrydelsen* to Veena Sud was its "unflinching look at the price of a life," its focus on the impact of the central killing on the family involved, as concentric circles of trauma and damage emanate from an act of violence.[3] This emphasis on the aftermath of crime allowed Sud to build on her experiences working as a producer on the earlier female-centered police procedural *Cold Case*:

> That was [*Cold Case* creator] Meredith Stiehm's vision when she created *Cold Case*, that we get to know the victim, we had to see them in every single flashback, we had to reconstruct their life and get to know them as human beings not just as a corpse in a body bag.[4]

This focus on the impact of crime even more than on the goal of identifying the killer is the first part of *The Killing*'s feminist challenge to the linear, problem-solving convention of the police procedural, the move from "whodunit" to "why do we care whodunit." But the killing of the teenaged Rosie Larsen also potentially implicates *The Killing* in another recurring trope of the crime narrative: the exploitation of the sexual violation and death of a young woman. A fixture of crime literature, movies, and television, the body of a dead young woman has become a persistent trope of visual narrative. Within the subgenre of the forensic procedural, such as *Bones* or especially the *CSI* franchise, the violated and exposed body of an attractive young woman is made the center of visual attention and literally the scene of investigation. Graphic forensic references to the details of sexual violation work both to stir moral outrage and to incite a transgressive curiosity, all the while reducing the victim's identity to her status as a sexually desirable body.

This is certainly the case with the killing of Nanna Birk Larsen in *Forbrydelsen I*, where the medical examiner provides Sarah Lund with the graphic details of the multiple violations of the teenager's body. The focus on the sex crime invokes older, reactionary views on women's sexuality—the idea of sexual violation as a "fate worse than death"—while it also subsumes the victim's identity and agency. When we later learn that Nanna had initially left home in order to run away with a boyfriend she thought her parents would disapprove of, *Forbrydelsen* again plays into an older cultural narrative that locates the original crime in the undisciplined sexuality of the victim.

While the Rosie storyline in *The Killing* does include Linden and Holder investigating whether Rosie's murder was connected to her romantic life as well as the plotline brought over from *Forbrydelsen* involving the possibility that Rosie worked for an online escort service, the initial coroner's report indicates that the time Rosie spent in the water had made any evidence of rape inconclusive, a point made almost as a throwaway line. What is emphasized instead are Rosie's efforts to claw her way out of the car trunk as it filled with water, raising the stakes in terms of Linden's emotional commitment to the case and stressing Rosie's active efforts to resist becoming a victim.

The care taken not to sensationalize the spectacle of Rosie's dead body is clear in the pre-credit opening to episode two of season one, "The Cage," as Rosie's working-class parents, Mitch and Stan Larsen (Michelle Forbes and Brent Sexton), arrive at the morgue to identify their daughter's body. Conducted entirely without dialogue, the scene features close-ups of the medical examiner carefully, even gently, removing Rosie's sneakers and taking her fingerprints with equal delicacy, as if not to disturb her. We never see a full shot of Rosie's body; instead we observe from outside the examining room as the sheet is lifted from her

43

The grief of Stan and Mitch Larsen after identifying their daughter's body. Rather than sensationalizing the violence of Rosie's death, *The Killing* focuses on the impact of violence on the Larsen family.

head and only her parents see what is beneath, their grief carrying the emotional power of the scene.

In the end, Rosie's motives were very different from Nanna's, and the series ends with an affirmation of her identity and meaning to her family. While Nanna's ambitions were stereotypically defined by romance, Rosie hoped to enact the abandoned ambitions of her mother to see the world. The title of the final episode of season two, "What I Know," is also the name of the eight-millimeter film that Rosie made to say good-bye to her family and tell them why she was leaving. After Linden secretly returns a videocassette copy to the Larsens, the family silently watches Rosie (Katie Findlay) express, via cue cards Bob Dylan–style from *Don't Look Back*, her optimistic desire to see the world and her love for her family. Rather than another troubled teen fleeing another dysfunctional family, a victim in the making, as prefigured in the Rosie-like runaway that Mitch attempted to befriend earlier in season two, Rosie defies the ultimate cynicism of the noir universe through her self-assertion, creativity, and kindness.

Forbrydelsen, in keeping with the classic noir tradition, consistently maintains an almost Calvinist vision of a fallen world, where venality and anger will always frustrate the search for justice and fairness, culminating in the conclusion where the father's desire to avenge his daughter's death results in him killing the killer, his thirst for vengeance trumping the need to keep the family together. The tragedy of the Rosie Larsen murder in *The Killing*, conversely, ends with an affirmation of the Larsens, despite their conflicts and struggles, as a functional and loving family. This Utopian note ultimately renders the murder of Rosie even more tragic; rather than another inevitable example of a fallen and irredeemable world, her death—ultimately not the result of a deranged killer but of political idealism and romantic fantasies gone terribly wrong—suggests a blow against a possible, better world. This glimmer of Utopian possibility in the brutal noir world of *The Killing* is all the more unsettling, countering the grim complacency of "well, what did you expect?" with the hint of a different outcome.

Resisting the Battle of the Sexes

This occasional glimpse of a better world recurs throughout all four seasons of *The Killing*, from the street kids moving into a subsidized apartment in season three to the final scene in the final season, where Linden abandons nihilism and returns to the Seattle she had previously seen as a "city of the dead." Perhaps most distinctively, this Utopian note also informs how *The Killing* radically revises the battle of the sexes model that has long defined male-female partnerships in the televisual police procedural. In *Forbrydelsen*, each season introduced a new male partner for Sarah Lund, and each became part of the conventional sexual tension model dating back to *Moonlighting*. In season one, Lund's married, equally "normalized" partner has to adjust to working with a powerful woman, emphasizing the anomalous woman angle. In seasons two and three, Lund's professional partners also become or once were romantic partners, the first turning out to be the killer who in turn tries to murder Lund, the second a former lover now married to another who is planning to leave his wife for Lund when the series ends on a disastrous note, with Lund executing the bad guy and fleeing Denmark into an uncertain future.

The Killing takes aspects of these various romantic intrigues and weaves them into strands of each season: season three combines the killer-lover and ex-lover plotlines—as well as the emergence of a serial killer—in the figure of James Skinner (Elias Koteas), Sarah Linden's former police partner who leads the task force investigating the murders of young runaways that he has really committed. Linden and Skinner do briefly reignite their relationship, and in another mash-up of plotlines from *Forbrydelsen*, Linden executes Skinner (who taunts her until she does so, in a scene based on the concluding episode of the first season of *Forbrydelsen*) and spends the final season trying to cover up her crime.

But even throughout the Skinner plotline, Linden's most significant relationship remains that with the partner she acquires in the first episode of season one, the former undercover narcotics officer turned homicide detective Stephen Holder. It is Holder who arrives just too late to prevent Linden from shooting Skinner, and it is Holder who becomes her co-conspirator in concealing the crime in season four, an enterprise that drives them apart and almost turns deadly before a final reconciliation that marks the most Utopian aspect of the series. A combination of colleague, sibling, confidant, and therapist, Holder from the start deliberately disturbs the standard will-they-or-won't-they sexualized paradigm that defines Sarah Lund's partnerships in *Forbrydelsen*.

The Danish original used a series of hypermasculine counterparts both to "balance" Lund's challenge to normative gender roles and to reinforce a fundamental gender binary and sexual normality. As Linda Mizejewski points out in her history of the

The character of the recovering addict Detective Stephen Holder (Joel Kinnaman) provides a voluble counterpoint to Sarah Linden's wary defensiveness and challenges the traditional gender dynamics of the police procedural.

woman detective in popular culture, "The possibility of . . . 'slip-page' from heterosexuality creates the need to appease one faction of the audience and tease another."[5] No matter how off-putting or emotionally distant Lund may seem, each of these partners continually reminds the viewer of her potential for sexual desire and desirability, containing her gender strangeness (and even potential queerness) within the familiar confines of the battle of the sexes. In short, men are incapable of being partnered with Lund—and, by implication, with any woman—without their relationship coming to be defined and even dominated by erotic attraction.

In Sarah Linden's partner Stephen Holder, played by the Swedish American actor Joel Kinnaman, *The Killing* introduces less a potential romantic partner and more another troubled child, an ex–undercover cop and (we eventually learn) a recovering addict whose contrast with Linden is based more on temperament than gender. "'I totally reconceptualized [Sarah Linden's partner] as a former undercover narcotics cop,'" says Sud, "'because I was just interested in these two clashing types—a deeply private, guarded homicide detective with a guy who's this chameleon with no boundaries.'"[6] Rather than the conventional performances of muscular, straight masculinity that defined Lund's partners in *Forbrydelsen*, Holder's performance of gender foregrounds the very idea of performance. Holder affects the street patois and hip-hop fashion sense of the "wigger," as the street kid Bullet mockingly describes him in season three, the white kid engaged in an unstable mimicry of black culture. Both a comic figure and a lost boy, Holder/Kinnaman quickly became a fan favorite, providing a voluble and hilarious contrast to Linden's tense stoicism.

From their first meeting in episode one, where à la *Forbrydelsen* Holder starts moving into Linden's office while she is still moving out, their relationship is defined by this clash. Throughout that initial scene, Holder makes no explicit reference to Linden's gender. Instead, he immediately begins to pry into her personal life, using the interrogator's technique of purposely presenting his target with inaccurate information (H: "So I hear you're moving to LA." L: "San Francisco area") in order to break down the instinctive wariness suggested by her vague reply of "San Francisco area."

Throughout the series, Linden and Holder don't so much talk as continue this interrogation, with Holder playing the voluble "good cop," Linden the cagey witness. Rather than flirty interplay, their dialogue is the professional banter of skilled practitioners, a cop version of playing the dozens that has served as the basis for male bonding in countless buddy movies and television shows. In this case, *The Killing* plays off the trope of the seasoned veteran testing/teaching/hazing the newbie, a dynamic made explicit when Lieutenant Oakes (Garry Chalk) sends Linden out to one last crime scene—the Rosie Larsen murder—points to Holder, and tells Linden, "Take him. Show him how to work a scene." In this reverse of expectations—throughout *The Killing* and especially in season one, Holder is continually trying to prove himself to Linden—*The Killing* demonstrates its complex awareness of the genre of the police procedural. While there may be no ultimate escape from genre expectations, either in a theoretical sense or in terms of the marketing realities of television programming, interesting things happen when those expectations are quietly turned inside out.

49

This understanding of genre expectations in *The Killing* means that the program doesn't ignore an erotic component between Linden and Holder or offer the pretense of a purely "platonic" relationship. While *The Killing* dramatically revises the relationship between Linden and Holder from *Forbrydelsen*, it keeps intact the professional/sexual relationship between mayoral candidate Darren Richmond (Billy Campbell) and his campaign advisor Gwen Eaton (Kristin Lehman) in the parallel political plotline of seasons one and two.[7] If anything, the contrast between the revisionist relationship of Linden/Holder and the more stereotypically melodramatic pairing of Richmond/ Eaton serves to heighten our awareness as viewers, Bertolt Brecht–style, of the ideological conventions at play in the melodramatic police procedural. This self-awareness can extend to our awareness of the erotic components at play in the relationships between any two of the characters, regardless of gender.

The reversal Sud refers to in her description of Linden and Holder—"deeply guarded" versus "a chameleon with no boundaries"—could imply a simple inversion of gender roles, with Linden as the stoic, emotionally wary "man" and Holder as the voluble, emotionally expressive "woman," that could grow increasingly tiresome over the course of a serial narrative. Instead, we can more usefully regard the development of Holder as providing a revision of masculine performance and identity. In the *Forbrydelsen* original, for all of its genre and gender revisionism in terms of the main female detective, the performances of masculinity remain stubbornly and generically conventional, reinforcing the character of Sarah Lund as an anomaly, a fish out of water.

Through Linden's partnership with Holder in *The Killing*, however, her assumption of a traditionally masculine genre and gender role works to revise those very codes of masculinity. Part of *The Killing*'s focus on the impact of violence on the family and community includes examining the costs of toxic masculinity, from the alpha males in seasons one and two to the psychopathic patriarch Skinner and the legacy of paternal violence represented by the falsely convicted Ray Seward in season three to the traumatized adolescent killer and the brutal military school culture of the final season. Holder's simultaneously evolving relationship with Linden, his struggles with rehab, and his efforts to repair the broken family relationships caused by his addiction represent a larger effort to redefine masculinity, to redraw the traditional generic binary of the battle of the sexes.

In playing with the conventions of police procedural masculinity and drawing on Sud's own interviews with actual undercover cops, Holder also crosses lines of race and class in his assumption of a wigger personality that verges on parody. His character exploits the idea of being "undercover," of constantly performing as an Other in a way that blurs the distinction between a "real" and "assumed" identity: "'Every single undercover that I met who has been wildly successful, [it] has been difficult to tell the difference between them and the bad guys.

They never went out of character ever because that's who they really actually were.'"[8]

The instability of the "chameleon"-like Holder's persona adds to both the mystery of *The Killing* and the viewers' reception of the series. His hip-hop performance verges on minstrelsy, and both Linden's character and fans of the show were kept guessing as to how "real" this performance was. Are we supposed to view him as "authentically" street, or is his performance deliberately over-the-top? On the one hand, he tells Linden in the first episode that he was immediately recruited into undercover work at the police academy, suggesting his performance of masculinity was already well-suited for the role. Or was it? There is a playfulness to Holder's performance that not only provides comic relief in the program but points to the character's own interest in experimenting with his "real" identity.

Throughout the series, Holder is involved in a process of self-reclamation and self-reinvention, combining hard-boiled habits and street smarts with an openness to New Age self-help. In contrast to Linden's classic taciturn noir demeanor, Holder is a compulsive chatterbox, constantly urging Linden to talk more about her feelings and relationships. Of course, this belief in the possibility of personal reinvention and redemption may be the most stereotypically "American" revision of *Forbrydelsen*. In any case, Holder's evolution over the course of *The Killing* allows for an equally evolving relationship between Holder and Linden, one that resists and revises traditional generic expectations for the partner dynamic in the police procedural, whether the single-sex "buddy" model or the eroticized battle of the sexes version.

In the end, breaking with *Forbrydelsen* by providing Linden with a single partner over the run of the series allowed Sud and her writing collaborators to play with the very idea and the ambiguity of the term "partner." Over the course of four seasons, the relationship between Linden and Holder becomes increasingly close and increasingly complex, culminating in a series conclusion that further baffled/frustrated fans who persisted in understanding male-female relationships in terms of a strict friend/lover dichotomy. As the relationship between Linden and Holder develops, they each become involved in romantic and sexual relationships, Linden with her former partner in season three, Holder with a lawyer in the district attorney's office, whom, in the space between seasons three and four, he marries, has a child with, and divorces.

The ending of the final episode of the final season fades to black, followed by the intertitle "Five Years Later" that introduces an epilogue. In the epilogue, Holder has left the force and his marriage, and we see him in a tender moment sending his young daughter off to preschool before beginning what is apparently his new career running the addiction recovery workshops we have seen him attending over the course of the series. Leaving the building, he is surprised by the arrival of Linden, who has been traveling the country, her son now in college. What follows is both a kind of confession and an articulation of the theme of family and community that define *The Killing* as a feminist revision of the police procedural: "I never had a house to grow up in . . . you know, home?" she tells him. "I never belonged anywhere. All my life I was looking for that thing, thinking it was out there somewhere."

She has returned to tell Holder that she realizes "maybe that home was us, it was you and me together in that stupid car. . . . I think that was everything. I'm sorry. I should have known that you were one person who always stays. You were my best friend." Holder responds, "Why don't you stay?" but Linden, seeing Seattle as a "city of the dead," finally turns and leaves. We then watch a montage of Linden driving through the city, concluding with her looking across the water at the Seattle skyline, a pose that reprises a similar one in the first episode and that became a visual trademark for the program, as well as evoking Rosie Larsen in her good-bye movie. We then cut back to Holder closing up the rec center where the rehab group meets and turning to see that Linden has returned. They approach each other as the camera pans away.

The dominant reading in the fan community was that this epilogue signaled a romantic relationship between the two, in classic melodramatic fashion. Sud did not disavow this interpretation when asked but instead answered ambiguously:

> There were many different possibilities for how the story of Linden and Holder would end. . . . From the very beginning, I knew that her journey would have to end in a place of uneasy peace, where there were no good guys, there were no bad guys. . . . I always knew that finding that peace would be an inner journey at the very end for her. Holder says, "It's not ghosts in front of you, it's not the dead." And that revelation of who is standing in front of her and who's in her life was something that I instinctually knew [I wanted to get to] from the very beginning. I didn't know it necessarily would be *Holder*.[9]

53

"I didn't know it necessarily would be *Holder*." Sud's disclaimer moves attention away from the specific teleology of the romantic relationship and back onto Linden's journey as lonely wolf to find that uneasy peace, to find the home that Linden points to as the defining desire in her life. We first encounter Linden in the series on her morning run, and Sud describes her character arc in terms of "finding the truth of what is in her life, and not running away."[10]

In the end, the question of what the future might hold for characters like Linden and Holder becomes a litmus test for viewers, a register of each viewer's investment in the conventions of genre and gender. Characteristically for this fraught series, the ending created complex divisions among fans, from those decrying a romantic ending as too trite or embracing it as wish fulfillment to the larger questions of whether what we are seeing really *is* the beginning of a romantic relationship and, crucially, just what "romantic relationship" means by the end of *The Killing*'s four seasons. When asked about rumors of a climactic kiss between Linden and Holder (apparently the actors improvised a kiss after the final camera pan away), Sud was clear in her determination to not be clear: "I knew I never wanted to film a kiss. That would have felt a little too pat."[11] For a series intent on revising the ethical focus, generic expectations, and gender conventions of the police procedural, a "pat" ending would never do.

The "Real Cost" of Murder

Family and Relationships in The Killing

The changes that Sud and her team made to *Forbrydelsen* in transforming it into *The Killing* provide the clearest insight into their revisionist orientation to the American police procedural. While a greater familiarity with the Danish original might have provided context for some of the critical and fan arguments about the first season of *The Killing*—and at the very least demonstrated just what a bold addition the character of Stephen Holder is to the narrative—in the end *Forbrydelsen* and *The Killing* both stand as exemplars of a turn toward televisual feminist noir. In the final chapter, I will discuss how the development of this and other subversive takes on classic television genres is being facilitated by the dramatic explosion of media distribution channels—the "disruptive" effect of digital technology, to use contemporary business jargon.

In this chapter, we will look closely at the four seasons of *The Killing*, seasons that in themselves present mini case studies of the creative instability of television in the digital age. From wrestling with the constraints of adapting a critically successful

European series in seasons one and two in order to establish a unique identity for *The Killing*, to a third season that seemed to promise an extended run on AMC only to end in cancellation, to a final resurrection as an over-the-top binge-watching experience on Netflix, *The Killing* compresses the history of entertainment television over the last twenty years. A show that both courted viewers and burned bridges with them, *The Killing* ultimately sacrificed longevity in lieu of intensity, providing viewing experiences that used the noir procedural conventions to continuously upend them, all the while building thematic through lines and points of connection that provide a coherent new take on the procedural. More focused on the consequences of violence than the parceling out of blame and punishment, on exploring a noir hero who longs for connection rather than romanticizing the social loner, *The Killing* ultimately dismisses world-weary cynicism in favor of the power of social connection. By the end of the four seasons of *The Killing*, the trope of the noir detective and criminal as mirror images of each other has been turned into a kind of social diagnosis, that violence results from the disintegration of connection and community, and that an open-ended reintegration, one not based on restrictive ideas of identity, gender, and sexuality but on acceptance and compassion, is the way to "solve" crime.

In what follows, I will outline how each storyline in *The Killing*—the killing of Rosie Larsen in seasons one and two; the search for a serial killer preying on homeless young people in season three; the investigation of the execution of a wealthy family in season four—appears to follow the formal guidelines of the noir-inflected police procedural only to transform the focus of each narrative away from the linearity of the thriller and toward an emphasis on family, community, and relationships, thus creating a procedural less focused on a linear obsession with "solving" crimes than with repairing the damage done: "But we're not spending time looking at a dead child's body and just analyzing that. We're spending time with all the people who have lost her, the impact of this loss on her mother, on her siblings, on her father."[1]

Seasons One and Two: Focus on the Family

> We said from the very beginning this is the anti-cop cop show. It's a show where nothing is what it seems, so throw out expectations. We will not tie up this show in a bow. There are plenty of shows that do that, in 45 minutes or whatever amount of time, where that is expected and the audience can rest assured that at the end of blank, they will be happy and they can walk away from their TV satisfied. This is not that show.
>
> —*Veena Sud*

For all of its innovativeness in creating the gender-stereotype-defying character of detective Sarah Lund, the first season of *Forbrydelsen* ultimately follows a conventional plotline: a young girl raped and murdered by a devious male serial killer, who in the end provokes the victim's father into executing him despite Lund's best efforts. This model engages in the cultural fascination with sexual violence against women even as the official narrative logic affirms the justice of capturing and eliminating the killer. More to the point, the serial killer narrative affirms the idea of violence as an external threat to the sanctity of the family and conventional society. *Forbrydelsen* does complicate this formula somewhat by making the killer a longtime employee of the Larsen family business and an uncle figure to the victim. Still, he remains a kind of infection, a stranger who becomes/impersonates the familiar.

The first two seasons of *The Killing* upend this insider/outsider logic, as the violence that kills Rosie Larsen and threatens her family can't ultimately be located in an outsider, whether the character of Belko Royce (Brendan Sexton III), the troubled Larsen company employee who is the counterpart for the killer in *Forbrydelsen*, the idealistic but ambitious politician Darren Richmond, or even the character who (almost) takes all the blame, Richmond's pathologically loyal campaign manager Jamie

Wright (Eric Ladin). The revelation in the last episode of season two that it was Rosie's beloved aunt Terry (Jamie Anne Allman) who sent the car with Rosie in the trunk into the water, all in an effort to salvage her doomed affair with wealthy developer Michael Ames (Barclay Hope), finally brings the violence back into the family itself and denies any simple notion of justice or retribution. No external punishment can be more harrowing than Terry's self-loathing, an interior guilt that bonds Terry to Rosie's mother, Mitch, and to Sarah Linden at the same time that the enormity of her crime forever alienates her from her family. At the end of season two, Terry is left in a comatose psychological state that mirrors the Sarah we saw falsely imprisoned in a psychiatric ward in the earlier episode "72 Hours." The Larsens are left with a multiple tragedy—the loss of a daughter/sister and a sister/aunt—that undermines by impossibly complicating any sense of linear closure or satisfaction that the mystery has been "solved" on the part of both the audience and detective Sarah Linden. The sardonic exchange between Holder and Linden from the series pilot—"At least you get the bad guy"; "Really? Who's that?"—comes back with tragic force at the end of the two-season Rosie Larsen story arc, forcing our attention back onto the "real cost" of murder.

Throughout season one, *The Killing* as adaptation plays a cat-and-mouse game with its original Danish source material, dutifully following some plotlines while subverting others, most notably in the character of Holder but also in increasing the focus on the social meaning and construction of motherhood as it relates to the "real cost" of murder. *The Killing* borrows the red herring strategy of *Forbrydelsen*—building up one potential solution, only to dramatically undo it to pursue another—but rather than using this plot device as a means of building suspense toward a final, satisfying solution, *The Killing* thematizes the concept of the red herring as a symbol of the impossible desire for clarity and closure. By ending season one with the biggest red herring of all, providing us with the mayoral candidate

Richmond as the killer only to take it back as Linden discovers that the supposedly conclusive photographic evidence implicating him was faked, *The Killing* radically and deliberately divided the fan community by forcing viewers to examine what exactly it is we want from a police procedural, including the ethics of the murder of young women as popular entertainment.

That some viewers felt cheated—that this final red herring was all a contrivance just to secure ratings for season two—is understandable given AMC's marketing strategy for their highly touted prestige drama. In an echo of ABC's *Twin Peaks* "Who Killed Laura Palmer?" campaign twenty years earlier, AMC promoted the show with the tag line "Who killed Rosie Larsen?" That parallel should have been a signal to viewers. *Twin Peaks* was much less interested in solving a mystery than in creating an increasingly eerie, surreal, and disturbing mise-en-scène for its shaggy dog narrative, and the "answer" to the question of "Who Killed Laura Palmer" likewise proved unsatisfying and even beside the point and ultimately led to the end of the series.

Similarly, although for very different cultural purposes, *The Killing*'s second season suggested that the desire for the narrative closure of the procedural may be the real red herring, that the cost of violence is not just more significant than the assignment of blame but that the whole idea of "assigning" blame can act as a way of trying to isolate and thus insulate ourselves against that violence. Still, throughout the first season, AMC—understandably from a marketing point of view—fed the desire for closure through an online fan environment that encouraged viewers to vote on who they thought the killer was and why, creating a kind of weekly stock exchange showing the changing percentages of the current suspect du jour. It's no wonder then that the final episode of season one, "Orpheus Descending," might be seen as a "ludicrous cliffhanger" by those expecting a more conventional police procedural.[2]

Yet the fans' frustration also mirrored the emotional arc of Linden's character, as throughout the first season we confronted

The question of just why she is so obsessed with this case, at the

the question of just why she is so obsessed with this case, at the cost of her relationship with her fiancé and possibly even custody of her son. "This is like the last time, when you got sick," her boss, Lieutenant Oakes, tells her in the first episode of season two, "Reflections," alluding to a mysterious prior case that led to an earlier breakdown and that will form the backbone of season three. Linden continues her emotional disintegration in season two, again frustrating viewers who wanted the show to remain focused on the murder puzzle but further developing the idea of the red herring in particular and detective work in general as a paradoxical search for the truth that equally functions as a means of evading a larger truth, the "real" cost of crime.

As it turns out, the key plot development in the "Orpheus Descending" episode at the end of season one is not Richmond's dramatic arrest and potential assassination or Linden's discovery of the faked photograph. It is Rosie's mother, Mitch Larsen, leaving her family, the culmination of her own season-long emotional disintegration. In a moving and wordless scene near the end of the episode, she observes from a distance her parents, her husband, Stan, and sister Terry flying kites on the beach with her two young sons, Tommy and Danny. Her expression in close-up registers her previously articulated concerns that the best thing she can now do for her children is to leave and protect them from her own agony, an action that parallels Sarah's fraying relationship with her son, Jack (Liam James), which results in Sarah sending Jack to Chicago to stay with his father in season two.

In short, throughout season one and especially season two, *The Killing* more and more abandoned the "main" story in favor of the "secondary" stories of Mitch's and Sarah's traumas as mothers. Throughout its four cycles, *Forbrydelsen* followed the traditional narrative construction of televisual storytelling, whether sitcoms or dramas, of having "A" and "B" plotlines, toggling between the central story of the murder investigation and a secondary narrative about political intrigue. *The Killing* at first maintained this same "A" and "B" structure but more and more converted the primary and secondary narratives into the (police procedural) murder mystery versus the (melodramatic) family trauma, and then switched their importance. The shooting of Darren Richmond at the end of season one, which leaves him paralyzed and in recovery throughout season two, likewise converts a political thriller into family drama focused on the complex familial and emotional relationships between Richmond, his lover/campaign advisor Gwen Eaton (who has her own fraught relationship with her father, a U.S. senator), and his surrogate son/friend/disciple Jamie Wright, whose own total dedication to Richmond almost results in Richmond's destruction.

The acclaimed "Missing," the eleventh of thirteen episodes in the first season, exemplifies this deliberate refocusing away from the puzzle plotline and toward the "real cost" of murder. The placement of the episode is crucial; Linden and Holder have determined that Rosie spent her last night at a local casino owned by the Wapi tribe, a major break in the case and the introduction of a whole new setting and plotline (one original to *The Killing* with no correlation in *Forbrydelsen*). At this moment, Sarah receives a call from her son's school saying that he has been absent for several days. When a worried and angry Sarah does not find him back at the motel that has formed their temporary home (and the lack of a stable home for Sarah and Jack is a recurring motif in *The Killing*, one that echoes Sarah's past in the foster care system and that foreshadows the plotline involving homeless teens in season three), she and Holder spend Day Eleven of the investigation in an increasingly frantic search for Jack, the search for Rosie's killer temporarily put on hold.

The episode accomplishes several purposes related to *The Killing* as revisionist feminist noir: it provides backstory for both Linden and Holder; it bonds Linden and Holder emotionally over their damaged pasts; and it reveals to the viewers (although not yet to Linden) Holder's own efforts to repair the damage done to his relationship with his sister and nephew resulting from his meth addiction. Most important, it solidifies the identity between Linden and the Larsens as parents faced with the inescapable emotional vulnerability represented by parenthood. Throughout seasons one and two, *The Killing* distinguished itself as a revisionist police procedural, and "anti-cop cop show," through its steady, careful, deliberately paced, and ultimately relentless foregrounding of the trauma inflicted on the Larsen family, a trauma that no amount of police work can ever address. In fact, the sense that the investigation is almost beside the point after the devastation of the original act of violence is deeply embedded in the emotional centrality of the "B" story.

As Holder chauffeurs Linden around Seattle, offering both his knowledge of student hangout spots gleaned from his undercover days and attempting to console his partner, they reveal their deepest psychic pain to each other. For Holder, this is his struggles with addiction and his investment in the ideology of the twelve-step process, especially the idea of accepting the limits of one's power to control events around them. When Holder tells Linden over a fast food lunch (for the intense Linden consisting of only a cup of coffee), "Some things you can't fix. Maybe they just stay broke," she mocks his embrace of canned self-help wisdom, but his words resonate in terms of both the Rosie Larsen case and their mission as detectives to find "the bad guys."

Linden later reveals both to Holder and to the audience her childhood bouncing from foster home to foster home after being abandoned by her mother, a psychic trauma that violates the masculine noir tradition by openly expressing the source of Sarah's psychological vulnerability and decisively breaking with Sarah Lund of *Forbrydelsen*, who is involved in a much more stereotypical relationship with a controlling middle-class mother. This revelation also leads to the first major conflict between the two partners, as Holder, characteristically thinking out loud, opines, "No wonder you ain't a pro at being a mom." This foregrounding of motherhood—and especially the difficulties and social stigma attached to working motherhood—is a deliberate feminist intervention into the procedural on the part of *The Killing*.

After Holder apologizes for his remark, they wind up at a park where Linden reminisces about Jack's early childhood before hearing a police report about the discovery of a slain boy Jack's age. In a scene paralleling Stan Larsen's appearance at the discovery of Rosie's body in episode one, Linden and Holder race to the crime scene, with Linden breaking through police lines as Stan tried to do. When we hear over the open police lines that the body has been identified as another boy, not Jack, we see Linden's most open expression of emotion in the four seasons of *The Killing*, collapsing in convulsive sobbing with relief and fear, again mirroring earlier reactions of the Larsens, particularly Stan's private breakdown in a gas station washroom in episode five, "Super 8." When Sarah discovers Jack waiting blithely outside their motel room door listening to music over headphones, she discovers that he had been with his father, who had abandoned the family shortly after Jack's birth.

The search for missing loved ones, the desire to protect and restore family, repeats in season two, allowing *The Killing* to break most decisively with *Forbrydelsen* as family, community, and human interrelationships become the dominant theme in the series. Again and again, the noir procedural narrative line of "Who killed Rosie Larsen?" is sidetracked (to those intent on finding the "answer") or replaced (in line with *The Killing* as "anti-cop cop show") by a focus on the need for human connections and the fragility of those connections.

The narrative and emotional arc of the "Missing" episode repeats in multiple storylines about the search for lost loved ones: in the mystery of Mitch's disappearance; in Mitch's attempts to mother a Rosie-doppelganger runaway she meets on the road, herself another missing child; in Holder's harrowing abduction and beating at the hands of the tribal police; in Linden's incarceration in a hospital psych ward after breaking into the tenth floor of the casino where Rosie disappeared; in the young gangster-in-training Alexi's search for his real father; in Rosie's search for her birth father; in the mystery of Darren Richmond's disappearance and suicide attempt. All of these missing-people scenarios carry echoes of Rosie's own disappearance, in terms of both the immediate violence of her abduction and what is revealed to be her own search for her place in the world. These multiplying plotlines, each stemming from the expanding complexity of family and personal lives of all the main characters, likewise point to how *The Killing* amplifies and foregrounds the subversive power of the melodramatic. Rather than closure, viewers encountered increasing emotional and psychological complications that had no clear solutions.

The echoes of Rosie's disappearance occur on the microlevel as well in season two. Holder is beaten and left for dead in the woods, and Linden's desperate search for him in the episode "Off the Reservation" mirrors the original search for Rosie, down to the use of police dogs and having the final clues provided by local children. Linden's own beating into unconsciousness on the tenth floor of the casino, along with Holder's frantic phone calls to her, directly parallels Rosie's own earlier panicked phone calls from the same location and Jamie knocking her out, both acts of violence and efforts to conceal evidence of a crime.

This repeated emphasis on and experience of loss maintained the emotional focus of *The Killing* on the "real cost" of murder, both the act itself and its consequences in terms of destroying the bonds of love and connection. Violence is a virus in *The Killing* that eats away at interpersonal connections. Significantly, it is only the invocation of the bonds of love and family connection that ever works against violence, as when Stan, coerced by threats of violence against his family into performing a hit for the gangster Janek Kovarsky (Don Thompson), is stopped by the sight of a baby in the car seat of the man he is supposed to shoot in the episode "Bulldog"; or when Holder convinces him in the final episode, "What I Know," not to physically attack his sister-in-law Terry after learning that she is responsible for Rosie's death by reminding him that his sons still need their father; or when, ironically, Stan learns in "Openings" that Rosie's love had saved his life as he could not save hers by dissuading Alexi (Tyler Johnston) from avenging his birth father's death at the hands of Stan twenty years earlier. These hedges against the darkness remain fragile and vulnerable to further betrayal, as when Alexi brutally murders Kovarsky, the man he had looked to as a surrogate father, after learning that he had ordered Stan to murder his father.

In addition to these literal desperate searches for lost loved ones in season two, the theme of abandoned and isolated children fully emerges as the emotional focus of *The Killing* and part of its radical revision of the noir police procedural, a focus that is even more fully developed in seasons three and four and that comes to stand as the essential symptom, the essential dysfunction, at the heart of the violence that drives *The Killing* as murder mystery. Sarah's backstory in the foster care system links her both to Alexi and to Adrian (Rowan Longworth), the child at the center of the case that led to her previous breakdown and who returns as the focal point of season three. Adrian was discovered trapped in an apartment for a week with his murdered mother; Sarah spent a night alone as a five-year-old in a dark, unheated apartment after her own mother abandoned her. Her history risks repeating itself in "Keylela," as she and Jack flee from Child Protective Services after Jack's father lodges a complaint. Sarah ultimately sends Jack to stay with his father in Chicago, a move that serves the narrative purpose of freeing her to focus on the Rosie Larsen case but that also reflects back on her own struggle with the cultural expectations of motherhood. The dysfunctional community of Seattle is symbolized by these legions of abandoned and lost children.

At the end of season two, however, *The Killing* breaks most decisively with both its immediate Nordic noir predecessor and the lone wolf noir tradition by refusing the utter bleakness of the end of *Forbrydelsen* season one, with Sarah Lund's partner dead and the Birk family in shreds after the father murders his daughter's killer. In some ways, the darkness of the ending of the Danish series depends on the greater sense of social cohesion in Denmark provided by a more robust welfare state than in the United States that both Danish creator Søren Sveistrup and Veena Sud alluded to. Similarly, although Sarah Lund is devastated by the loss of her partner and final act of killing, she remains embedded in a more secure family structure and social safety net. Sarah Linden, on the other hand, becomes literally homeless in *The Killing*, and her partner Stephen Holder is not a married family man (as in *Forbrydelsen*) but a recovering meth addict trying to regain the trust of his sister and nephew.

That *The Killing* stresses the vulnerability of family and community raised the stakes in terms of the impact of violence in the show and its critique of the lone wolf noir hero. Throughout the first two seasons, the lonely wolf detective Sarah Linden has to confront her need for and dependence on others, not as a weakness as in the noir tradition but as a source of strength and stability. Her obsessive pursuit of justice links with her empathic connections to the isolated victim. She constantly repeats how alone Rosie was in the woods, especially when she realizes that had Rosie only made a different turn when fleeing from her killer, she would have found the lights of a neighborhood. Community and family, however flawed, mean safety, or at least the closest approximation of it, in Linden's worldview, a safety that was denied her in her own childhood and that she has a conflicted relationship with as an adult.

This compensating knowledge, however attenuated or fragile, is echoed in the title of the final episode from season two, "What I Know." As we have already discussed, the title is taken from the film that Rosie Larsen made to say good-bye to her family before leaving to follow the migration of the monarch butterflies. "What she knows" is that the world is big, that she wants to see it, and, crucially, that she loves and has the love of her family. The episode begins by returning to the day Rosie

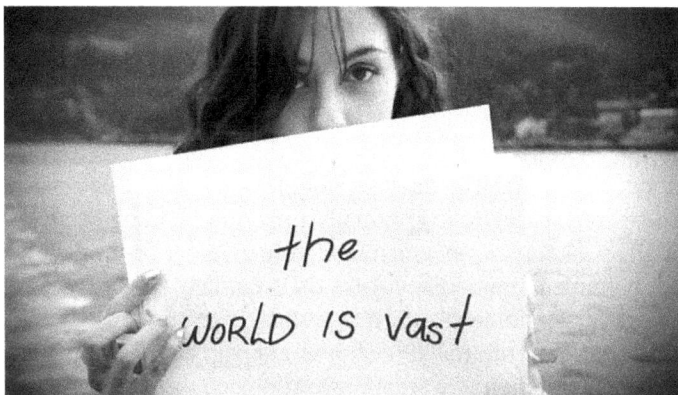

Although season one of *The Killing* began with her murder, Rosie Larsen is very much alive in her final appearance at the end of season two, providing a hard-won sense of hope and possibility with her film "What I Know."

disappeared, the last happy morning of the Larsen family. We see Rosie roughhousing with the boys while Mitch is distracted by last-minute packing for the family camping trip. They have a typical parent-teenager exchange before Rosie leaves for school, with Mitch reminding her to be home on time after the dance that night. It's a frazzled good-bye, followed by Rosie looking at Stan across the garage as he argues on the phone before she leaves. Earlier, Stan had confided to Rosie's friend Sterling that he remembered how sad Rosie looked as she walked out the door, worried that her expression signified a deep unhappiness.

Beginning and ending the final episode of the "Who killed Rosie Larsen?" case with the living Rosie is startling. As viewers, we have come to regard her as simply the victim, or in Alfred Hitchcock's sense the MacGuffin, an excuse to set the procedural plot in motion. Seeing Rosie alive brings us back to the "real cost" of murder by returning Rosie's agency and identity to her. Our final scene of the Larsen family finds them seated in front of the television, smiling and weeping at the images of a joyful, loving Rosie. This scene is not one of any simple "closure," however. It follows closely the revelation that it was not the happenstance outsider Jamie who is solely responsible for Rosie's death but her beloved aunt Terry acting more out of desperation than malice, herself another "lonely wolf" terrified about her future. The director Patty Jenkins, who also directed the pilot for *The Killing*, visually links the opening sequence with the later scene in which Linden and Holder confront Terry, as the camera ominously patrols the seemingly empty hallways of the Larsen home, horror-movie style. In the first case, we are relieved when the tracking shot is interrupted by the playing Larsen children; in the second, we approach the door to Rosie's room, inside of which we find the distraught Terry.

The final scene with the Larsens, then, works not to assure us that the family will recover or that love will conquer all but simply to reinforce the importance of connection, however vulnerable or fragile. The final scene of the episode concludes with Linden and Holder again in (or trapped in) the car, receiving a new assignment to investigate a body found near the airport. Rather than continue on her crusade, Linden silently exits the car and, we assume, her career. She and Holder have the same sardonic exchange about the ultimate value of police work—and by extension the police procedural genre—"We got the bad guy." "Yeah, who's that?" With that, Holder bids her good-bye—"Hey, keep in touch. You're my ride"—before driving off, leaving Linden staring at the outside of the Larsen home before she begins walking away.

Because the program was slated to be canceled, "What I Know" was originally meant to function as the ending to the series.[3] The cancellation was widely seen as a consequence of the program's failure to provide a conclusion at the end of season one, as borne out by declining ratings throughout the second season. What happened next points to the rapid changes in the television industry in the digital era that we will explore further in chapter 4. While AMC was ready to jettison *The Killing* in search of higher ratings, Fox Television, the producers of the series, was finding financial success with international distribution of the show. Negotiations between AMC and Fox, along with a strong pitch for season three from Veena Sud, led AMC to reverse course and bring back *The Killing*, along the way making a deal with Netflix to stream the episodes after they first aired on cable.[4]

So what had begun as an object lesson in the risks involved in crafting an "anti-cop cop show" instead turned into a second chance for a distinctive program with a strong point of view and identity, even if that identity included arguments about whether the program should be seen as bold and risk-taking or arrogant and dismissive of audience concerns. Clearly, *The Killing* benefited from appearing at a moment in the historical development of television when the criteria for what constitutes a "successful" program, while always fluid, were particularly in flux.

69

Season Three: Family as Found

Freed from the constraints in seasons one and two to follow, in however broad an outline, the structure and narrative of *Forbrydelsen*, season three of *The Killing* featured a more cohesive storyline centered on the mysterious case alluded to in seasons one and two that had led to Linden's earlier breakdown. The A and B storylines of season three shift between the search for a serial killer preying on young homeless women living on the streets of Seattle and the imminent execution of the prisoner Ray Seward (a star turn for the actor Peter Saarsgard), who had been convicted of killing his wife, Trisha Seward, after being apprehended by Linden and her former partner James Skinner, now the head of a special investigative task force. While Sud and her writing partners no longer had to maintain the connection to the overall story arc of *Forbrydelsen*, they nevertheless continued to riff on elements from the Danish series.

The third season of *The Killing* takes on the serial killer narrative that it had rejected in its first two seasons, offering an "anti-cop cop show" critique of the starkly gendered conventions of the serial killer procedural at a time when other prestige programming, such as Showtime's *Dexter* and NBC's highly aestheticized *Hannibal*, likewise indicated a growing self-consciousness about the serial killer genre in the digital era. Rather than following the lead of the conventional serial killer plotline by focusing the narrative on the duel between the intrepid detective and a charismatic evil genius killer, however, *The Killing* continued to emphasize the "real cost" of murder by concentrating instead on the community of homeless teens who are struggling to forge their own sense of family on the streets and in the shelters of Seattle. Rather than merely a convenient source of victims for the crime narrative, these young people acquire agency and identity in contrast with the institutional anonymity of the orange body bags in which the killer places them.

The breakout performance of this season was Bex Taylor-Klaus as the homeless lesbian teen Bullet, a character who came to define the moral center of the narrative and one of the most tragic examples of the real costs of crime, whose own efforts at hard-boiled street smarts and emotional vulnerability provided a counterpart to Linden's conflicted noir hero. Like Linden, Bullet tries to protect her small group of close friends—both her best friend, Kallie, and Lyric, the girl she loves—while maintaining an outward veneer of toughness and anger. She and Holder form a close bond in the search for Kallie after her disappearance sets the main narrative line of season three in motion. Bullet becomes for Holder what Rosie Larsen and Adrian were for Linden, and her death at the hands of the killer after a fight between Holder and Bullet leads him to his own dark night of the soul, with Linden comforting him and resisting his momentary leaning in for a kiss.

In effect, Holder becomes a father figure in season three, both to Bullet and later in "Six Minutes" to the young Adrian in the prison waiting area the day of his father Ray Seward's execution. In fact, in the style of the melodrama, families of

The parental bond and sense of identification that Detective Holder forms with the street kid Bullet (Bex Taylor-Klaus) reinforces the focus on society as family that defines *The Killing*.

various configurations—families of birth, of choice, of temporary exigency—form the heart of season three of *The Killing* and create a transition between the feminist revision of *Forbrydelsen* in seasons one and two and the family tragedy at the heart of the final mini-season. As with seasons one and two, the real threat in season three is not the monster without—the rogue serial killer—but a status quo that tolerates scores of children sleeping on the streets. "Human garbage. No one cares"; this statement is offered by both Pastor Mike (Ben Cotton), who runs a homeless shelter for street kids (and who becomes a red herring suspect in the crimes), and the real killer, Linden's former partner and lover James Skinner, as a descriptor of the characters we come to know as Bullet, Lyric, Kallie, and Twitch. While Pastor Mike's use of the terms is meant to signal his moral outrage at social apathy and Skinner's to excuse his string of brutal murders, they both acknowledge the matter-of-factness of the situation, one Linden herself existed on the fringes of as a troubled foster child prone to running away.

All of the major characters in season three are depicted as members of family groups: the street kids who look out for each other (in particular the characters of Lyric and Twitch [Julia Sarah Stone and Max Fowler], who acquire a subsidized apartment and try to create a new family); the main victim, Kallie Leeds (Cate Sproule), and her distracted single mother, Danette (played by the indie film star/director Amy Seimetz); the condemned prisoner Ray Seward and his son Adrian; the prisoners who share death row; the prison guards Francis Becker (Hugh Dillon) and Evan Henderson (Aaron Douglas); James Skinner's disintegrating nuclear family and his resumed relationship with Sarah Linden; Holder and his new partner, the veteran Carl Reddick (Clark Gregg); and Holder and his girlfriend, District Attorney Caroline Swift (Jewel Staite).

Just as season two of *The Killing* expands the focus on the Larsen family to foreground the conflicts and complexities of mothering, season three continues this emphasis through the bond forged between Linden and Danette Leeds, at whom Sarah first registers disgust over Danette's seeming callous lack of concern for her missing daughter. The two gradually form a bond that extends to the families of missing girls who come to the police station wondering whether any of the bodies found at the killer's watery dump site (one of many echoes of the Rosie Larsen case in season three) might be their daughter. Danette's doomed efforts to locate Kallie eventually lead her to both Bullet's funeral and then a poignant scene in "From Up Here" with the runaway Lyric, who is trying to escape turning tricks on the street by working in a fast food restaurant, offering Danette a chance to provide parental support to another lost child.

These extending lines of maternal connection proliferate throughout the season to incorporate the prime oedipal tension of fathers and sons as well. Over and over, characters are presented with parent-child scenarios and opportunities, and our estimation of them is largely defined by how well we feel they occupy these roles. The serial killer investigation in season three follows a deliberately clichéd list of masculine pathologies found in traditional police procedurals: a creepy clergyman with a shadowy past who ministers to the homeless teens; a mama's boy with a taste for pedophilia; a death row inmate with unresolved oedipal conflicts who may or may not have murdered his wife. Yet in each case, a common thread emerges that connects this collection of "outsiders," including the eventual killer, Lieutenant James Skinner.

In their own ways, each of these suspects is at heart a struggling father. Pastor Mike, the street minister with a mysterious past, tries to find meaning by serving as a protector of homeless teens. Joe Mills (Ryan Robbins), who will eventually wind up taking the rap for the killings in season four, preys on these same teens for sexual fulfillment but wins Danette's trust by playing on her loneliness and feigning a paternal interest in Kallie. Ray Seward, the falsely condemned killer who has followed his own father's path into a life of violence and prison, ultimately wants his son to have a different, better life. Even Skinner, the brutal killer of dozens of young women, justifies his actions through a perverse reading of his duties as a father, seeing his actions as virtually mercy killings: "I save them," he tells Linden, from their status as "human garbage."

"I have been alone for too long, and so have you," Skinner tells Linden in the same episode, "The Road to Hamelin," the final episode in the season, as he drives them to his lake house on the pretense that he has imprisoned Adrian there, the boy Linden longs to protect and who turns out to have witnessed Skinner as the Pied Piper killer. "You and I are nothing alike," Linden angrily answers, but in fact season three repeatedly reinforces not only that likeness but her kinship with virtually every other major character on the show, whether on the basis of struggling single parenthood or of being a throwaway child herself, or by trying to escape the psychological prison of her own emotional guardedness and distance.

To care for children, however, to recognize the inevitable connections of community and family, whether those connections are based in genetics or a sense of duty and responsibility, is the ultimate counter to the attractions and pathologies of the lone wolf. *The Killing* uses the character of Skinner to draw the ultimate correlation between the lone wolf noir hero and the lone wolf serial killer, a parallel that again is expressed in other revisionist procedurals such as *Dexter*, where the lone wolf detective is also a serial killer, and one whose ultimate undoing and redemption is effected through loyalty to his son.

When Linden accuses Skinner in "The Road to Hamelin" that killing Adrian was his real objective the night he murdered Trisha Seward, Skinner attempts to defend himself—and reveals more of his pathological understanding of fatherhood—by claiming, "I don't kill children." "They were all children," Linden angrily replies, meaning specifically the homeless young women he had murdered but by extension everyone in the world. The condemned prisoner Ray Seward becomes the child he was when he confronts his inmate father in "Eminent Domain." His cellmate, Alton (Little JJ), is himself barely a legal adult, convicted of killing his own parents in a botched robbery, leading to his guilt-stricken suicide. Seward's tormentor, the prison guard Francis Becker, is a failed father who tries to impress his own young son with the gallows under construction, only to find his son a murderer after shooting the lover of Becker's wife.

At the end of "The Road to Hamelin"—and thus the end of season three—*The Killing* again plays off of *Forbrydelsen*, in this case the conclusion to the Danish series as a whole. In the case of *Forbrydelsen*, Sarah Lund, bitterly frustrated that she is unable to apprehend the child killer she has been pursuing because of his extensive business and government connections, turns executioner and murders him. Her partner/lover helps her leave the country, and the series ends with Lund on an airplane, leaving Denmark and her family seemingly forever. In *The Killing*, Linden murders Skinner after he taunts her into doing so (an echo of the end of *Forbrydelsen I*), but not because she lacks evidence to convict him. Instead, it is her own implication in his pathology—her love for him, and by implication her own desire for connection and intimacy—that frightens her. She does not flee the country, however; the season deliberately ends on a cliffhanger that holds out the prospect for another season.

"It's the loneliest thing in the world, waiting to be found," Linden expresses more to herself than to Skinner in "The Road to Hamelin" after he suggests that there may be multiple dump sites containing the bodies of lost children who will never be found by their distraught parents. Linden's words recall her pain at thinking of Rosie's terrified run through the woods in seasons one and two, and they explicitly refer both to the search for the missing Kallie and to the story told by Danette of Kallie's inability to understand hide-and-seek as a little girl. Danette would close her eyes and count to ten, but when she opened her eyes Kallie would always be standing right in front of her. In "From Up Here," the penultimate episode of season three, we see Danette on the bridge where we first meet Bullet and Kallie, closing her eyes and counting to ten, hoping that her daughter will appear again when she opens them. "We never stay and in the end we lose everyone," Holder tells Linden near the conclusion of "Six Minutes," the episode detailing the lead-up to Seward's execution. Holder's Zen-existentialist summary of the fragility and vulnerability of life stands in tension with Seward's poignant memory of his son's childhood, "when they still think the world is big," a memory that connects back to Rosie's film from the end of season two.

In the end, season three of *The Killing* is about the inevitability and necessity of building family—both family as inherited and family as found—in the face of these unsettling realities, as Holder moves into new models of paternal care and as motherhood—especially a tension between "bad" mothers and the need to redefine the maternal—continues to be foregrounded. Instead of sending the lone wolf hero off alone into an uncertain but isolated future as at the end of *Forbrydelsen*, season three of *The Killing* ends with Linden and Holder together by Skinner's body at the lake house. Whatever the next steps may be, the connection between Linden and Holder endures, as Linden's question about the search for a "bad guy"—"really, who's that"—implicated rather than simply frustrated viewers of the show, as we need to calibrate our own understanding of the generic conventions of the police procedural in relation to our investment in the questions of justice and vengeance—and, most important, the question of the "real cost" of murder—in relation to the actions of Linden and Holder. They are questions that animate the narrative of the final, streaming-based "season" of *The Killing*.

Season Four: The One Who Stays

> From the very beginning, I knew that her journey would have to end in a place of uneasy peace, where there were no good guys, there were no bad guys. There was a truce that she had to make with the world as it is versus the way she wanted the world to be.
>
> —*Veena Sud on the conclusion to* The Killing

> I should have known that you were one person who always stays.
>
> —*Sarah Linden to Stephen Holder, "Eden"*

Season two of *The Killing* had seen a drop-off in ratings that initially led AMC to cancel the series before a deal between AMC, Fox Television, and Netflix brought the show back for season three. While season three maintained the ratings (approximately 1.5 million viewers a week) of season two, AMC again decided to cancel *The Killing*. Fox Television persisted, this time leveraging the streaming deal with Netflix into a fourth and final season made available for immediate binge-viewing. This final reprieve allowed Veena Sud, along with her main writing and producing partners, Dawn Prestwich and Nicole Yorkin, to bring the series to a deliberate conclusion, one that affirmed the program's milestone status as a revisionary feminist police procedural.[5]

The final season of *The Killing* takes place in the hothouse environment of tandem dysfunctional houses: the sleek steel-and-glass postmodern showcase home of the wealthy Stansbury family, whose bloody massacre is the instigating crime for the season, and St. George's military academy, a neo-Gothic school for the troubled sons of Seattle's richest families and home to main suspect Kyle Stansbury (Tyler Ross). The school is presided over with an iron fist by another hard-boiled female noir character, Colonel Margaret Rayne (Joan Allen in another casting coup), who turns out to be one more troubled mother futilely trying to save her son, the same Kyle she had given up for adoption seventeen years before. All the while, Linden's relationship with Holder becomes increasingly strained as they attempt to cover up her execution of her ex-lover turned serial killer at the end of season three.

The six episodes of season four bring together all of the revisionist thematic strands of the first three seasons—the focus on lost children in a dysfunctional social order; the epic existential responsibility of parenting, family, and friendship—to create a hard-won, embattled, but nevertheless Utopian ending that defies the dark, gendered cynicism of the traditional noir procedural. In the end, the idea and ideal of staying, of avoiding the desire to run, away from both the entanglements of community and connections and the inescapable burdens of the past, becomes the moral touchstone that underlines the "real cost" of murder and defines *The Killing* as anti-cop cop show.

In season four, the killers are both perpetrators and victims, as Linden and Kyle Stansbury have to confront and acknowledge their acts of violence, even as that violence can only be understood as embedded in larger webs of family violence and social dysfunction. *The Killing* ultimately rejects the "whodunit" reductionism of the conventional police procedural as well as the crime-and-punishment model on which it is based. Kyle Stansbury, the obvious suspect, who is found at the crime scene covered in blood and unconscious as the result of an apparent botched suicide attempt, turns out in fact to be the killer, although not the bad guy, not the "monster" he feared he had become. It is the stories surrounding the crime, the cruelties, secrecies, and conspiracies that attempted to maintain a pretense of normality, that reveal "who cares whodunit," in the case of both the murdered Stansburys and the murdered serial killer James Skinner. In the end, there is no running away from these stories, just as there is no "sending away" our lost children, whether to prison, to a military school, to a father in Chicago.

As Sud insists, the goal of *The Killing* is the decidedly unnoir-like "uneasy peace," along with the reintegration of the lonely wolf Sarah Linden into the bonds of friendship and family, and the arcs of the narrative lines of season four challenge our own generic expectation of viewers as we calculate episode-to-episode just how and whether Linden and Holder will avoid the discovery of their actions in season three, and more to the point whether they *should* avoid that discovery and the potentially devastating consequences that could result.

The themes of abandonment and isolation, of disconnection from family and community, that have defined *The Killing* as revisionist noir from the start multiply in the final season. Kyle Stansbury was "abandoned" by Margaret Rayne, his birth mother, who tried to parent from afar by spying on him as he grew up in the abusive Stansbury family and later futilely attempted to shield him from the consequences of his crime as the commander of his military school. Sarah confronts the birth mother who abandoned her and gave her up to the foster care system. Sarah wrestles with her own abandonment of Jack, who returns for a spring break visit only to find his mother again distracted and distant, anxious over the prospect of the further abandonment represented by her arrest and conviction for Skinner's killing. Holder's own fears of arrest compound his terror of failing at his own prospective parenthood. Danette Leeds, the mother of the murdered Kallie Leeds from season three, searches for solace as she continues to deal with her guilt and grief over abandoning her daughter to the streets. At the conclusion of "Eden," Sarah faces abandoning yet another child, in this case Kyle, whom she clings to as another emotional surrogate following her obsessions with Adrian Seward and Rosie Larsen. As she realizes that Kyle did in fact murder his family, including his beloved six-year-old sister Nadine, her own predicament collapses into Kyle's, as she wrestles with whether to help him get away.

All these cases of abandonment reinforce the social critique inherent in Sud's declaration that "we live in a society that is incredibly violent."[6] In *The Killing*, the issue Sud raises as a result—"So the biggest challenge is to make us, as Americans, care about this young girl over a long period of time"— encompasses both the difficulty of creating an emotionally compelling narrative that evokes the "real cost" of murder and a social landscape that makes care, whether in the form of parenting or police work, almost impossible. These instances of seeming abandonment can also be read—or rationalized—as self-sacrifice, of parents "saving" their children from the wrecks of their own lives by running away.

In the fourth episode of the season, "Dream, Baby, Dream," Holder asks Linden (of all people) for parenting advice in his typically blunt fashion (and demonstrating how *The Killing* took advantage of the loosening of language censorship brought about by the move to Netflix): "How do you do it? How do you not fuck them up?" Linden's answer evokes what becomes the ultimate foundation of the "uneasy peace" she and Holder achieve at the end of the season and the end of the series: "You just do your best. You're here. That's what matters. It's kind of the only thing that matters. You show up." "Showing up," of course, refers to the fundamental action of detective work, an act of diligence and faith that transcends any particular outcome of any individual case. It also acts as a decisive rebuttal of the noir lone wolf, at the levels of both ethics and social theory. Running away does not alter the inevitable interconnectedness of social relationships. Rather than a source of fear over the loss of autonomy found in the androcentric noir tradition, these relationships become the source of salvation for Linden.

Linden's advice is echoed by Danette Leeds, another of the structurally isomorphic mothers—Sarah Linden, Regi Darnell, Mitch Larsen, Margaret Rayne—who shift the moral center of the noir procedural away from masculinist isolation toward the recognition of connection, dependency, and vulnerability. "I just don't want to fuck it up," Holder repeats in "Eden," this time to Danette at Kallie's grave, where he has come to apologize and give her Kallie's earring. "Then don't," Danette answers, bluntly framing the ultimate ethical and moral question at the heart of *The Killing*. "I know what it's like to walk away, how hard it is to stay," Linden tells Margaret Rayne, bonding with yet another mother in pain.

After Kyle's confession and arrest, Linden follows suit, admitting her murder of Skinner to Detective Reddick while exonerating Holder. What happens next is straight out of the more conventional noir ethos of *Forbrydelsen* as well as an expression of the covert melodramatic foundation of the noir tradition. Mayor Darren Richmond shows up to explain to Sarah that the revelation of a highly ranked detective as a serial killer would be too damaging to the reputation of the police force and by implication his tenure as mayor. Skinner's death will be officially listed as a suicide, and blame for the crimes will remain with the pedophile Joe Mills.

It is in the context of this deeply cynical resolution that the "Five Years Later" epilogue to "Eden" is important not just as a tacked-on "happy ending" but as a final refutation/revision of the conventional noir procedural. For some viewers, "*The Killing* is as close to nihilism as TV gets: It's not there to offer hope for mankind or even for its characters."[7] Yet to read *The*

The impossibility of parenting: Stephen Holder and Danette Leeds (Amy Seimetz) meet over the grave of Kallie, her murdered daughter.

Killing's focus on the "real cost" of crime, its careful depiction of the ramifications of violence and murder on the families and communities that experience them, as a form of "nihilism" is to remain embedded in the noir logic of running away, that the exploration of this pain can only lead to hopelessness. Yet as Rosie Larsen's movie in "What I Know" expresses, the Larsens remain enriched by the legacy of Rosie's hopefulness, her sense that "the world is still big."

"The most important thing to me is not to pornographize murder . . . I want to show the real cost . . . when a child is lost."[8] Rather than nihilism, Sud's mission statement for *The Killing* from season one becomes the basis for the "uneasy peace" of the epilogue. "There is no bad guy. There's just life," Sarah tells Stephen, before admitting, "I should have known you were one person who always stays." As we discussed in the previous chapter, while many viewers were quick to assume a romantic union between Linden and Holder, Sud insisted, "I knew I never wanted to film a kiss. That would have felt a little too pat." Too pat and too much. Instead of a kiss or even an embrace, we only see that Sarah has returned to Stephen after initially leaving (again). There is no kiss, no embrace, no words. We only see a smile from Sarah and a fade to black. In the end, it's staying that embodies the hard-won victory over nihilism. "It's the only thing that matters," Sarah had told Stephen. "You show up." At the conclusion of *The Killing*, that remains the only thing that matters.

From Cable to the Web

The Killing *as Cult TV in the Digital Age*

On January 10, 1999, the cusp of the new millennium, *The Sopranos* debuted on the premium cable channel HBO. *The Sopranos* was not HBO's first effort at original programming, but the overwhelmingly positive critical reaction to the show, as evidenced by 21 Emmys and 111 nominations during its eight-year run, including Best Drama in 2004, the first time a non–broadcast network program had won that award, signaled a sea change in the traditional business and programming models of broadcast television.[1] Eight years later, on July 19, 2007, the first episode of *Mad Men* appeared on AMC, a basic cable channel, after being turned down by both HBO and Showtime.[2] Its similar critical success to that of *The Sopranos*, including a lock on the Best Drama Emmy for its first four seasons, all on a basic cable channel, further eroded the hegemony of the big four networks.

If *The Sopranos* and *Mad Men* were harbingers of the radically changing contours of that massive and amorphous cultural formation we call "television," the appearance in 2013 of *House of Cards* on Netflix—neither a broadcast network nor a cable channel but a web site—decisively signaled that a new era in television history had begun. Like HBO, Netflix is a subscription service, but unlike both HBO and AMC it requires neither a cable/satellite contract nor even a television set to access. Part of the move to "over-the-top" (OTT) web streaming, Netflix, Amazon, and other web-based companies have transitioned from being archives and repositories for programming that originally appeared on a "network" like CBS or AMC to competing directly with these other content providers, while also still providing access to their programs.[3]

These three televisual milestones exemplify the rapidly evolving and even revolutionary television environment in which *The Killing* was developed, produced, and made available for viewing. *The Killing* appeared at and benefited from this critical time in the history of television in the digital age, especially the move from cable to web-based, OTT programming. By premiering just as streaming services like Netflix and Amazon were beginning to produce original programming, *The Killing* turned what was most problematic about the series from a traditional marketing point of view—its tendency to polarize audience reactions—into a potential strength.

Both AMC's decision to renew the series after its controversial first two seasons and its later decision to drop it after season three point to the ongoing negotiation broadcasters and distributors have faced in the digital era between the longstanding industry practice of trying to create the broadest audience possible for a program and the powerful loyalty generated by the smaller but often demographically attractive niche viewers. OTT programming has built on this niche-viewing trend to create a moment when the intensity of viewer interaction has replaced traditional ratings as a possible measure of business success. From this perspective, *The Killing* represents a case study in terms of the evolution of the business model for commercial television, its cult status a defining characteristic of OTT programming.

Sarah Linden and Stephen Holder, always in the rain.

This destabilizing of the traditional television business model and traditional models of television viewership has also facilitated a move toward feminist television represented by shows like *The Killing* and other contemporary women-centered police procedurals. As binge-watching moves from the fringes to a normalized mode of television viewership, historically conventional ideas of what is meant by a "TV series" face potentially revolutionary changes. In its resistance to the linearity of the police procedural, *The Killing*, a series defined by Sud's commitment to "slow-burn storytelling" in the service of an "anti-cop cop show," anticipated the binge-watching model of OTT services, a model that built on the earlier binge-watching culture of DVD viewing.[4]

While the tendency of any new format or delivery system is to imitate existing industry models of programming, these new viewership models have created a space for just the kind of experimental counterprogramming represented by Sud's deliberately feminist revision of the traditional noir-inflected police procedural. As we saw in chapter 1, the history of women in the police procedural during the first decades of network television mainly featured versions of "fish out of water" narratives focused on the character of the anomalous woman. When an intentionally feminist rewrite of the procedural was attempted in the case of *Cagney and Lacey*, the production history was fraught with network anxiety over implications of lesbianism and other potentially "radical" implications of that groundbreaking series. The result was the sporadic appearance of highly compromised experiments, exceptions that proved the rule of the dominant broadcast genres and practices.

In contrast, the last ten years have seen a wave of feminist interventions into televisual conventions, especially on cable networks and streaming services, from comedies such as *Broad City* and *Unbreakable Kimmy Schmidt* to dramedies like *Orange Is the New Black* and *Transparent*. The metaphor of a wave, of course, is relative; anything approaching gender equity in terms of content and production practices is still far from reality across the broad range of what we now call "television."[5] Still, in comparison to the glacial progress before the new millennium, this recent opening up of the televisual landscape to feminist revision is striking. The new viewership and business models that have been emerging since the turn of the century point to a move away from the mass-audience model toward niche-viewing communities defined more by viewer loyalty and superviewer enthusiasm than traditional rating numbers.

From TV III to Matrix Media

That the history of television has always been that of a medium in a constant state of transition has become a commonplace of media studies. One shorthand model posits three key periods in that history: TV I, the era of broadcast television that lasted until the early 1980s; TV II, the period marked by the emergence of cable television and the proliferation of TV channels; and TV III, or television in the digital age beginning in the 1990s, with the explosion of web-based, streaming, and other digital services. That this last period implies a more revolutionary transition in television history than the first two, one that challenges our fundamental understanding of what we even mean by the term "television" (and by extension television studies), can be seen in the titles of the recent essay collections *Television after TV* and *Television Studies after TV*.[6] Indeed, the move toward OTT and streaming services like Amazon and Netflix has (inevitably) led some scholars to suggest that we may have entered TV IV.[7]

Television scholar Michael Curtin has proposed "matrix media" as a useful metaphor for making sense of what is happening to television in the digital age. Instead of linear models based on a traditional production-distribution-consumption structure dependent on a finite number of access points— channels and networks in the TV I and TV II models—matrix media describes an environment where viewers can interact with programming through an ever-expanding array of experiences: "It was no longer a broadcast medium or a network medium, or even a multichannel medium; television had become a matrix medium, an increasingly flexible and dynamic mode of communication."[8] Rather than a medium based on a limited number of programs and a resulting reliance on building the highest ratings possible, television is entering a period of abundant programming and specialized audiences: "The definitions among TVI, TVII, and TVIII rest broadly on notions of channel scarcity versus channel abundance and of broadcasting to a mass audience versus narrowcasting to niche audiences."[9]

For revisionist programs like *The Killing*, and for the fostering of revisionist feminist programming in general, there are two main implications resulting from the development of television in the age of matrix media. One is an emerging business model that can provide new structures of financing and profit for alternative programming within the constraints of capitalist media. The other stems from the increasing importance and relevance of niche audiences and community building in an era being constructed on the emergence of OTT streaming services and binge-watching viewing practices. Rather than only transitory experiences within the ceaseless flow of network programming and commercials, television programs in the digital era have acquired a cultural status more akin to literature, as texts can be extracted from any particular channel, any particular network flow, to be endlessly viewed, reviewed, written about, and incorporated into fan fiction, mash-ups, and other user-generated content. An exemplar of the kind of programming that used to be known as "cult TV," *The Killing* emerged at a time when the cult went mainstream—or rather, when the mainstream is transforming into an array of cults, niches, and communities.

88 The Escape from Ratings: New Business Models in the Digital Age

The history of *The Killing*'s survival over the course of four seasons is a case study of the changing business model of television programming in the digital era. *The Killing* started as part of AMC's expansion into original programming, in keeping with the erosion of the main broadcast networks' monopoly on original programming over the last thirty years. But *The Killing* also reflected the changing contours of the global television market. Fox Television, the production company behind *The Killing*, was looking not just to import and sell to the U.S. market a proven success in the European market—the Danish series *Forbrydelsen*—but also to potentially exploit that same international market for dark crime dramas with a noirish police procedural set in the United States that could then be exported back into those same markets.

The result was the introduction of multiple profit models that could be used to measure the financial success of *The Killing*, but models that were themselves evolving within the changing dynamics of matrix media. In deciding whether to renew *The Killing* for a second season, AMC relied on the traditional television business model of viewer ratings, albeit in the context of a greatly diversified viewing environment that was constantly recalculating what might be considered a "good" ratings number. Prestige and cultural buzz also played a role in ways even more difficult to translate into numerical equivalencies in deciding to order another season of the critically acclaimed series.

The polarizing conclusion to season one created greater network anxiety over season two, and when the ratings numbers declined from those of season one, the traditional expectation would be that *The Killing* would be canceled. While AMC was calculating viewership numbers, however, Fox Television saw that *The Killing* was finding just the international audience they had hoped for, potentially trumping the importance of its U.S. ratings performance. At the same time, the negotiations between AMC and Fox Television were taking place in the context of what had emerged since the 1990s as a lucrative aftermarket for television programming on streaming services like Amazon and Netflix. More and more, in fact, these OTT services were less an aftermarket than another market, progressing toward a situation where programs would appear simultaneously on "network" channels and on OTT services, services that were themselves creating their own original programming.

The deal that enabled a surprise third season of *The Killing*— a joint deal among AMC, Fox Television, and Netflix—was prescient in terms of the emerging business models of matrix media. From there, the move to a Netflix-only final season, available all at once *House of Cards* style with no commercial breaks and no restrictions on language, could have been seen as less of a surprise than an expectation. In this way, streaming became divorced from "the flow" of traditional broadcast television.[10] *The Killing* as a programming entity existed apart from a channel, apart from a network. A series that began as part of AMC's strategy to build a network brand associated with edgy, dramatic programming by the end had drifted free of AMC, carrying its community of fans with it.

In writing about the impact of *The Sopranos* on the television business model, Mark C. Rogers, Michael Epstein, and Jimmie L. Reeves credit HBO "for its pioneering efforts in introducing first-order commodity relations to the commercial television landscape."[11] By "first-order commodity relations" they mean a model where programming is sold directly to viewers rather than having a program serving mainly as a lure to attract eyeballs to television advertising. As a premium cable channel, HBO was less interested in viewer ratings per se than in maintaining and growing their list of subscribers, subscribers who would choose HBO on the basis of the programs themselves. Their business model was more like that of the movie industry, with viewer subscriptions the equivalent of ticket sales, or as Tim Wu suggests in imagining a television future dominated by Internet-based streaming services, "Ultimately they're all just selling access to piles of content to be perused at the viewer's desire. Oddly enough, it's a vision that actually makes television a lot more like the rest of retail."[12]

And like Hollywood in the age of the classic studio system, premium channels like HBO and Showtime as well as the advertising-dependent basic cable channels like AMC and USA that were competing with them as sources of innovative original programming began to build brand identities. "It's Not TV, It's HBO" and "USA: Characters Welcome" were the equivalent of MGM's reputation for high production glamour or Warner Brothers' association with urban realism in the 1930s and 1940s. As Curtin argues, this new, studio-brand style of television production "not only reflects changes in audience use patterns, but also points to changes in the ways that programs are conceived, financed and executed. As one executive put it: 'We have to manage for profit margin and not for ratings.'"[13]

For *The Killing*, this new first-order commodity emphasis proved crucial in keeping the series alive. Instead of an older business model of trying to maintain enough first-run ratings to produce eighty to one hundred episodes that could later be syndicated onto local channels as a continuing source of revenue, the combination of international sales, DVD/Blu-ray packages, and streaming services provided an immediate source of profit that could justify continued production after just a single season. While *The Killing* initially fit into AMC's branding strategy based on adult-oriented hourlong dramas, its move onto Netflix (following the earlier, pioneering example of the cult comedy *Arrested Development*) marked *The Killing*'s separation from any particular network brand identity and its recognition as a cult favorite based on the program itself. In this model, viewers did not go to AMC to look for interesting programming; they instead followed the programming to wherever they could access it. In fact, leaving AMC only strengthened *The Killing*'s identity as "auteurist" television or, as Roberta Pearson aptly puts it, "cult television as digital television's cutting edge."

From Fragmentation to Community: *The Killing* and Feminist TV

From a formalist and aesthetic point of view, the move away from ratings-based, network programming and toward an existence as a first-order commodity cult program connected to a loyal viewership has important implications for a revisionist program like *The Killing* in general and feminist television in particular. While a conventional wisdom has emerged that connects the move toward TV III (or IV) and the metaphor of "matrix media" with greater and greater audience fragmentation and potentially isolation, this fragmentation can also be read in terms of a growing capacity for "community-based" programming that can provide opportunities for new voices and perspectives to enter what is still a mass medium of televisual programming, a potential that connects *The Killing* both to other feminist revisionist procedurals such as *Top of the Lake* and to a larger community of feminist genre revisions, from *Orange Is the New Black* to *Transparent* to *Jessica Jones*.

In his introduction to the essay collection *Television as Digital Media*, James Bennett acknowledges both dimensions of television in the digital era. While observing that "the transition to television as digital media is about the rise of a digital culture that increasingly both networks and atomizes society,"[14] he qualifies this cautionary note by pointing out that while "television's era of mass audiences may be increasingly called in question, its digital formation continues to facilitate new and important forms of community."[15] Any concerns about the "atomizing" effect of the digital era likewise risk romanticizing the social unity supposedly associated with the broadcast era of TV I, as John Hartley astutely points out:

> Broadcast television was always a mixed blessing, displaying at once the positive and negative aspects of a regime of semiotic and political representation in which common, generalized experience was represented on screen and in legislatures by professional expert elites (actors and politicians, *mutatis mutandis*). So *everyone was represented*—ordinary life and everyday choices were the real "platform" of mass media—but simultaneously *no one spoke for themselves*. Everything was realist but nothing was real.[16]

Atomization versus community, homogenizing narratives versus revisionist experiments aimed at a more authentic or at least alternative realism; these contrasts both speak to the contemporary landscape for televisual programming in the digital era and define the main thematic obsessions of Veena Sud's "anti-cop cop show" *The Killing*. The revisionist emphasis on "the real cost of murder" speaks to Hartley's description/critique of traditional televisual narrative as a place where "everything was realist but nothing was real." As we have seen, this "real cost" in *The Killing* has to do with the opposition between atomization and community, between isolation and the inevitability and indispensability of interdependence.

In the case of *The Killing*, however, this atomization is not presented as a rupture brought about by digital technology with a supposedly more integrated society of the past. Instead, *The Killing* locates this atomization and fragmentation within the masculine-centric ideology of classic noir structure, the lone wolf narrative that valorizes the isolated (male) hero. From this perspective, the digital age can be faulted not for introducing social fragmentation and isolation but for insufficiently combatting it or even exacerbating it. Significantly in season four of *The Killing*, the tragically isolated teenage killer Kyle Stansbury is pointedly not immersed in online culture, nor does he even seem to own a smartphone. Instead he is embedded in the most traditional and patriarchal of institutions, a military school that sets itself in deliberate opposition to contemporary culture, down to the level of the ballroom dancing lessons that represents Colonel Margaret Rayne's only leisure activity.

The Killing, then, does not ground its critique of the violence and anomie of contemporary American culture in a reactionary evocation of a less confusing past defined by clear social and gender roles. There is no nostalgia for a lost tradition of masculine honor and chivalry that haunts the noir fictions of a writer like Raymond Chandler. The past in *The Killing* is a place of abandonment, violence, and secrets, the traditions of St. George's military academy a cover for sadism and brutality. While the Internet can be a place of danger and exploitation, as in the plotline concerning the online Beau Soleil escort service in seasons one and two, digital technology also works as a means to create connections and community, particularly in the complex use of mobile phones as both investigative tools and lifelines of connection between Linden and Holder.

The creation of niche programming, then, that began with the proliferation of cable channels in the 1980s can likewise signal fragmentation for some, a chance for community and "speaking for oneself" for others:

Unlike the mass television era, when the industry churned out inoffensive mass-appeal programming, executives during the multichannel transition began to pursue groups of viewers who were passionate about particular ideas, topics and interests. These niches were constituted as much by their audiences' shared world-views as they were by their sense of difference from other viewers.[17]

After reminding us that "the whole idea of one great entertainment medium that unites the country isn't really that old a tradition, particularly American, nor necessarily noble," Tim Wu echoes *The Killing*'s revisionism by pointing out that

community lost can be community gained, and as mass culture weakens, it creates openings for the cohorts that can otherwise get crowded out. When you meet someone with the same particular passions and sensibility, the sense of connection can be profound. Smaller communities of fans, forged from shared perspectives, offer a more genuine sense of belonging than a national identity born of geographical happenstance.[18]

From the perspective of narrative form, *The Killing*'s move from the (still) advertising- and ratings-based model of AMC to the on-demand, niche-based cult TV communities of Netflix allowed for greater continuity and less fragmentation, for a more holistic viewing and storytelling experience. As Mareike Jenner puts it, "If television is defined less through the technology used and more through formats (particularly, it seems, the format of serialized drama) and we can schedule it ourselves, then the way to ask for our attention changes significantly. In other words, increasingly complex narrative structures demand our attention in a way scheduled television rarely can."[19]

The Killing's Veena Sud agrees: "On Netflix, each episode is longer because there are no commercial breaks, so the intensity

of the storytelling is nonstop, which is something that every sto-
ryteller loves—not to have to go to commercial break and sell
Tide to your viewers."[20] She points out that the move to Netflix
allowed for a greater "intensity" of viewing experience, an in-
crease in "richness and depth and nuance. It's like a 13-hour
movie, really."[21] While this interview was given in a context of
promotion-speak, Sud's description accords with the ways that
the narrative and viewing experiences on OTT services like Netflix are challenging even the basic terminology of the television
program.

For example, throughout this book, I have referred to the
four "seasons" of *The Killing*, drawing on a nomenclature and
exhibition practice as old as television itself. In the age of TV
I, network seasons seemed almost as predictable as the climate
seasons. New shows rolled out in September (often during a
"premiere week"), and prime-time programs all took a summer
hiatus, when the airwaves would be filled with reruns and summer replacements. This model was never as stable as it seemed,
of course. Competition soon created the midseason rollout, and
the advent of multichannel cable and satellite programming beginning in the late 1970s undermined the hegemony of fall as
the beginning of the network year.

Today the concept of "season" has divorced itself almost
completely from the calendar chronology. While a vestige of
the fall premiere season continues to signal the beginning (or
at least "a" beginning) of prime-time network programming,
actual start dates vary from the end of summer to after Thanks-
giving. Cable and satellite programming, on the other hand,
use the term "season" to refer to any related grouping of a single
program, regardless of the calendar. The reality show *America's
Next Top Model*, for example, managed to fit twenty-two "seasons" into its twelve-year history, while a year and a half sepa-
rated "seasons" four and five of *Mad Men*. For *The Killing*, its first
three seasons followed a standard practice of thirteen episodes
apiece, although as we have seen the show's decision to extend

the narrative line of season one through season two disturbed many in the fan community, essentially creating a twenty-six-episode season not that much longer than the twenty-episode first "season" of the Danish original *Forbrydelsen*.

The move to Netflix was a move from a thirteen-episode season three to a six-episode season four, but as Sud alluded this change also encompassed a radically different approach to each episode. Like a premium cable program, the episodes no longer had to follow the narrative beats dictated by commercial breaks; like cinema, the chronological change from an episode per week to the immediate availability of the entire "season" allowed for greater continuity and information density and eliminated the need for a "previously on *The Killing*" prologue.

With its constant availability online as well as what we might now think of as "traditional" DVD and Blu-ray discs, *The Killing* as cult TV remains forever available as part of the virtually limitless catalog of online OTT services. In a sense, *The Killing* has never been canceled, any more than we can say that the novel *David Copperfield* was "canceled" because Charles Dickens stopped writing about that group of characters. Part of the moment within the history of television that *The Killing* inhabits has meant that the program has never left screen availability, even beyond the emergence of DVD collections of popular television shows at the turn of the century.

All of these business and formal developments—the emergence of television programs as first-order commodities no longer solely dependent on network distribution; the move toward viewing communities based on shared values and interests; the growing dominance of the over-the-top model of distribution—have allowed for the emergence of "the cohorts that can otherwise get crowded out" that Wu refers to in terms of the growth of revisionist "feminist" programming across old TV, cable, and OTT services. *Orange Is the New Black*; *Transparent*; *Girls*; *Inside Amy Schumer*; *Broad City*; *Unbreakable Kimmy Schmidt*; *The Killing*; *The Fall*; *Top of the Lake*—these and other revisionist programs represent less a coherent movement than groups and networks of like-minded creators taking advantage of a changing media environment in which the average of 5.2 million viewers who tuned in to watch Tina Fey's *30 Rock* on NBC in the 2010–11 season—good for 106th place among network programs—constitute a viable and valuable cult niche audience in the digital era.[22]

No one spoke for themselves. In putting together *The Killing* as an "anti-cop cop show" that would not "pornographize murder" and focus instead on a feminist understanding of the "true cost of murder," Veena Sud and her production team created a landmark program that serves as a decisive response to the critique and challenge posed by John Hartley to the mass representationalism of the first era of broadcast television. As significant as and in fact inextricable from *The Killing's* feminist revision of the noir police procedural is its representative status in terms of the potential for television in the digital age to challenge the frustrating endurance of sexist imbalance in television production, the celluloid ceiling that has blocked the entry of proportional numbers of women into production, direction, showrunning, and writing. It is no accident that revisionist feminist noir programs like *The Killing* and *Top of the Lake* that have emerged in the era of digital and OTT programming feature women auteurs—Sud and Jane Campion—as the creative and production drivers behind them.

Conclusion

> From the very beginning, I knew that her journey would have to end in a place of uneasy peace, where there were no good guys, there were no bad guys. There was a truce that she had to make with the world as it is versus the way she wanted the world to be. I always knew that finding that peace would be an inner journey at the very end for her.
>
> —*Veena Sud*

The story of a classic noir detective that turned the cultural logic of noir upside down, a police procedural less interested

"You and me, together in that stupid car." The relationship between Sarah Linden and Stephen Holder challenged viewer expectations of a traditional romance.

in whodunit than in why we should care, *The Killing* over the course of its forty-five episodes both infuriated fans and developed a loyal cult following that has inspired countless Pinterest pages, Tumblr sites, and thousands of words of fan fiction. The program has proved a landmark in its specific revision of the police procedural, in its participation in the larger cultural development of feminist noir, and in its emergence at a particular revolutionary moment in the development and very meaning of television. Its status as an early masterpiece in the era of OTT programming will ensure its continuing historical and cultural significance, but its more intangible elements—Mireille Enos's haunted look, the at once both familiar and radical easy banter between detectives Linden and Holder, and above all its deep-seated compassion and empathy in a genre known for neither—will keep viewers returning to a rainy Seattle where the sun finally shines at the end.

Introduction

1. For a representative sampling of love/hate reactions to *The Killing*, including critics and writers who claim the show angers and frustrates them but who still can't stop watching, see Appelo, Blake, Peitzman, and Stelter.
2. There is a vast scholarly literature on masculinity in film noir; see especially Krutnik.
3. Warner and Schmidt.
4. Gledhill provides a collection of essays that reflect the range and complexity of feminist appraisals of the melodrama. For a succinct early version of the case for the soap opera as potentially subversive women's narrative, see Modleski.
5. Strachan, 4.
6. Ausiello, 1.
7. Goldman.

Chapter 1

1. Littlefield, 1.
2. Callaghan, 1.
3. I treat the issue of the anomalous woman in greater length in the first chapter of *Masculinity in the Contemporary Romantic Comedy: Gender as Genre*.
4. "For a character as nonconformist as the woman detective—a woman whose story doesn't lead to love and marriage—the easiest way to assure audiences she's straight is to glamorize her, give her a male cop partner, or put her into a bikini and high heels, as television did with Angie Dickinson in *Police Woman* (1974–78), with plenty of silhouette-profile shots" (Mizejewski, 5).

5. Title VII of the 1964 Civil Rights Act, outlawing gender discrimination in hiring practices, began having a dramatic effect on the number of women in police work, beginning around the time of *Police Woman:* "In the United States, women constituted 1.4 percent of all police officers in 1971, 5 percent in 1980, 8.6 percent in 1990, and 10.6 percent in 2000" (Bellknap, 516). According to the U.S. Census, as of 2010 the number was 14.8 percent ("How Do We Know?").

6. Maerz, 1.

7. Ibid.

8. Anthony, 2.

9. Chozick, 1.

10. Lederman, 1.

11. Appelo, 1.

12. Emily Nussbaum refers specifically to the politics of non-linear storytelling in her review essay of Jane Campion's *Top of the Lake*, a review that also references Sud's "left brain/right brain" quote: "Campion's way of dramatizing crime is hypnotic and circular—we understand a few of the case's facts before the detective figures them out, and so the audience's 'gotcha' impulse to solve the puzzle and be done with it is circumvented" (4)

13. Chandler, 197.

14. Nussbaum, 4.

Chapter 2

1. See especially Collins.

2. Collins, 10.

3. Porter, 1.

4. Callaghan, 1.

5. Mizejewski, 9.

6. Porter, 2.

7. Since appearing as Gwen Eaton on *The Killing,* Kristin Lehman has gone on to star as a brash homicide detective herself on the Canadian series *Motive.*

8. Gee, 1.

9. Ausiello, 2. Emphasis original.

10. Ausiello, 2.

11. Ibid.

Chapter 3

1. Strachan, 4.
2. Blake, 3.
3. Hibberd.
4. Adalian.
5. Aurthur.
6. Strachan, 4.
7. Peitzman, 4.
8. Strachan, 4.

Chapter 4

1. "The Sopranos."
2. Handy.
3. Hall.
4. Goldman, 1.

5. See the annual reports on the progress (or lack thereof) toward gender equality in movies and television from the Center for the Study of Women in Television and Film at San Diego State University (Lauzen) and the Media, Diversity, and Social Change Initiative at the University of Southern California (Smith, Choueiti, and Pieper).
6. Spigel and Olsson; Turner and Tay.
7. Jenner.
8. Curtin, 13.
9. Pearson, 107.
10. The concept of analyzing broadcast television in terms of the ceaseless "flow" from program to commercial to news break to program derives from Raymond Williams's Television: Technology and Cultural Form. The move from "flow" to "streaming" in the digital era retains the hydraulic metaphor but points to a radically different kind of televisual experience.
11. Rogers, Epstein, and Reeves, 46.
12. Wu, 9.
13. Curtin, 16.
14. Bennett, introduction, 4.
15. Ibid., 9.
16. Hartley, 21. Emphasis original.
17. Curtin, 11.

18. Wu, 10.
19. Jenner, 269.
20. Ng, 2.
21. Ibid.
22. "2010–11 Season Broadcast Primetime Show Viewership Averages."

BIBLIOGRAPHY

Adalian, Josef. "Sorry, Hate-Watchers: AMC Had Three Good Reasons to Un-Cancel *The Killing*." *Vulture*, 24 January 2013. www.vulture.com/2013/01/why-amc-decided-to-bring-back-the-killing.html.

Alberti, John. *Masculinity in the Contemporary Romantic Comedy: Gender as Genre*. London: Routledge Research, 2013.

Anthony, Andrew. "The Killing: Meet Sofie Gråbøl, Star of the Hit Danish Crime Thriller." *The Guardian*, 12 March 2011. www.theguardian.com/tv-and-radio/2011/mar/13/the-killing-sofie-grabol-sarah-lund-interview.

Appelo, Tim. "'The Killing' Showrunner Responds to Finale Backlash: 'I Don't Want to Be Kinda Liked.'" *Hollywood Reporter*, 22 June 2011. www.hollywoodreporter.com/race/killing-showrunner-responds-finale-backlash-204728.

Aurthur, Kate. "Netflix Has Renewed 'The Killing' for a Fourth Season!" *Buzzfeed*, 30 July 2013. www.buzzfeed.com/kateaurthur/the-killing-ratings-renewal-chances-amc#.pnXnY4QEQw.

Ausiello, Michael. "*The Killing* Post Mortem: EP Veena Sud Talks That Last Scene, the Lost Kiss, an Offscreen Wedding and . . . a Season 5?" *TVLine.com*, 7 August 2014. http://tvline.com/2014/08/07/the-killing-season-4-spoilers-final-6-episodes-linden-holder-kiss.

Baym, Nina. "Melodramas of Beset Manhood: How Theories of American Literature Exclude Women Authors." *American Quarterly* 33.2 (1981): 123–39.

Bellknap, Joanne. *The Invisible Woman: Gender, Crime, and Justice*. Stamford, CT: Cengage, 2014.

Bennett, James. Introduction to *Television as Digital Media*, ed. James Bennett and Niki Strange, 1–27. Durham: Duke University Press, 2011.

103

Bennett, James, and Niki Strange, eds. *Television as Digital Media*. Durham: Duke University Press, 2011.

Blake, Meredith. "*The Killing*: 'Orpheus Descending.'" *A.V. Club*, 20 June 2011. www.avclub.com/tvclub/the-killing-orpheus-descending-57743.

Callaghan, Dylan. "Softly, With Her Song: With Her New Hit AMC Show *The Killing*, Veena Sud Takes Her Lifelong Fascination with Strong Female Characters in Dark Places to a New, Long-Form Level." *Writers Guild of America West*. www.wga.org/content/default.aspx?id=4599.

Chandler, Raymond. *The Big Sleep*. Reprint. New York: Vintage Crime/Black Lizard, 1988.

Chozick, Amy. "Something's Rotten in Seattle—AMC's New Series 'The Killing,' Imported from Denmark, Brings Nordic Noir to TV." *Wall Street Journal*, 25 March 2011, D4.

Collins, Laura. "Danish Postmodern." *New Yorker*, 7 January 7 2013, 22–30.

Curtin, Michael. "Matrix Media." In *Television Studies after TV: Understanding Television in the Post-Broadcast Era*, ed. Graeme Turner and Jinna Tay, 10–19. London: Routledge, 2009.

Gee, Catherine. "Interview: Writer Veena Sud on Her Remake of *The Killing*." *The Telegraph*, 6 July 2011. www.telegraph.co.uk/culture/tvandradio/8621343/Interview-writer-Veena-Sud-on-her-remake-of-The-Killing.html.

Gledhill, Christine, ed. *Home Is Where the Heart Is: Studies in Melodrama and the Woman's Film*. London: British Film Institute, 1987.

Goldman, Eric. "*The Killing* Brings Murder to AMC." *IGN*, 10 January 2011. www.ign.com/articles/2011/01/10/the-killing-brings-murder-to-amc.

Hall, Gannon. "Why 2011 Is Being Called the Year of 'The Cable Cut.'" *Business Insider*, 30 December 2010. www.businessinsider.com/what-will-it-take-to-make-over-the-top-video-successful-2010-12.

Handy, Bruce. "Don and Betty's Paradise Lost." *Vanity Fair*, 4 August 2009. www.vanityfair.com/news/2009/09/mad-men200909?currentPage=1.

Hartley, John. "Less Popular, But More Democratic? *Corrie*, Clarkson, and the Dancing *Cru*." In *Television Studies after TV: Understanding Television in the Post-Broadcast Era*, ed. Graeme Turner and Jinna Tay, 20–30. London: Routledge, 2009.

Hibberd, James. "'The Killing' Cancelled by AMC." *Entertainment Weekly*, 27 July 2012. www.ew.com/article/2012/07/27/killing-canceled.

"How Do We Know? America's Changing Labor Force." *United States Census Bureau*, December 2012. www.census.gov/library/infographics/labor_force.html.

Jenner, Mareike. "Is This TVIV? On Netflix, TVIII and Binge-Watching." *New Media & Society* 18.2 (2016): 257–73.

Krutnik, Frank. *In a Lonely Street: "Film Noir," Genre, Masculinity*. New York: Routledge, 1991.

Lauzen, Martha M. *Boxed In: Portrayals of Female Characters and Employment of Behind-the- Scenes Women in 2014–15 Prime-time Television*. Center for the Study of Women in Television and Film at San Diego State University, 2015. http://womenintvfilm.sdsu.edu/files/2014-15_Boxed_In_Report.pdf.

Lederman, Marsha. "Why *The Killing's* Veena Sud Is Drawn to Darkness." *Globe and Mail*, 15 June 2011. http://license.icopyright.net/user/view FreeUse.act?fuid=MjAyMDc2Njk%3D.

Littlefield, Kinney. "Veena Sud: Be Ready." *The Writer*, 30 September 2014. www.writermag.com/2014/09/30/veena-sud-ready/.

Maerz, Melissa. "Women as Partners in Crime Dramas." *Los Angeles Times*, 10 April 2011. http://articles.latimes.com/print/2011/apr/10/entertain ment/la-ca-crime-feminine-20110410.

Mizejewski, Linda. *Hardboiled and High Heeled: The Woman Detective in Popular Culture*. New York: Routledge, 2004.

Modleski, Tania. "The Search for Tomorrow in Today's Soap Operas: Notes on a Feminine Narrative Form." *Film Quarterly* 33.1 (1979): 12–21.

Ng, Philiana. "'The Killing' Boss on Netflix Revival, F-Bombs and Ending the Story (for Real This Time)." *Hollywood Reporter*, 31 July 2014. www.hollywoodreporter.com/live-feed/killing-veena-sud-netflix-f-72 1848.

Nussbaum, Emily. "Deep Dive: The Meditative Beauty of Jane Campion's 'Top of the Lake.'" *New Yorker*, 25 March 2013. www.newyorker.com/magazine/2013/03/25/deep-dive.

Pearson, Roberta. "Cult Television as Digital Television's Cutting Edge." In *Television as Digital Media*, ed. James Bennett and Niki Strange, 105–31. Durham: Duke University Press, 2011.

Peitzman, Louis. "'The Killing' Comes to a Close with a Colossal Mistake." *Buzzfeed*, 4 August 2014. www.buzzfeed.com/louispeitzman/the-kill ing-comes-to-a-close-with-a-colossal-mistake#.aiq1JoD7Da.

Porter, Rick. "'The Killing': EP Veena Sud Tries to 'Upend' the Cop-Show Format." *Zap2it.com*, 1 April 2011. http://zap2it.com/2011/04/the-kill ing-ep-veena-sud-tries-to-upend-the-cop-show-format.

Rogers, Mark C., Michael Epstein, and Jimmie L. Reeves. "*The Sopranos* as HBO Brand Equity: The Art of Commerce in the Age or Digital

Reproduction." In *This Thing of Ours: Investigating "The Sopranos,"* ed. David Lavery, 42–57. New York: Columbia University Press, 2002.

Sepinwall, Alan. "Interview: 'The Killing' Producer Veena Sud." *Hitfix*, 29 March 2011. www.hitfix.com/blogs/whats-alan-watching/posts/inter view-the-killing-producer-veena-sud.

———. "Interview: 'The Killing' Showrunner Veena Sud on the Season Finale." *Hitfix*, 19 June 2011. www.hitfix.com/blogs/whats-alan-watching/posts/ interview-the-killing-showrunner-veena-sud-on-the-season-finale.

Smith, Stacy L., Marc Choueiti, and Katherine Pieper. *Inclusion or Invisibility? Comprehensive Annenberg Report on Diversity in Entertainment.* Media, Diversity, and Social Change Initiative at the University of Southern California, 22 February 2016. http://annenberg.usc.edu/pages/~/media/ MDSCI/CARDReport%20FINAL%2022216.ashx.

"The Sopranos." *Emmys.* www.emmys.com/shows/sopranos.

Spigel, Lynn, and Jan Olsson, eds. *Television after TV: Essays on a Medium in Transition.* Durham: Duke University Press 2004.

Stack, Tim. "'The Killing': Exec Producer Veena Sud Spills Secrets on TV's New Hit Mystery." *Entertainment Weekly*, 17 April 2011. www.ew.com/ article/2011/04/17/the-killing-executive-producer-secrets.

Stelter, Brian. "Arts, Briefly; AMC Chief Responds to 'Killing' Complaints." *New York Times*, 27 June 2011, C3.

Strachan, Alex, "Making *The Killing.*" *OttawaCitizenDotCom*, 17 January 2011. www2.canada.com/ottawacitizen/news/artslife/story.html?id=6 8d0783d-c88f-4db7-a976-90138bb42aae.

Turner, Graeme, and Jinna Tay, eds. *Television Studies after TV: Understanding Television in the Post-Broadcast Era.* London: Routledge, 2009.

"2010–11 Season Broadcast Primetime Show Viewership Averages." *TV by the Numbers*, 1 June 2011. http://tvbythenumbers.zap2it.com/2011/06/ 01/2010-11-season-broadcast-primetime-show-viewership-aver ages/94407/.

Warner, Kristen, and Lisa Schmidt. "Reconsidering *The Killing* as a Feminine Narrative Form." *Flow*, 7 July 2011. www.flowjournal.org/2011/07/re considering-the-killing/.

Williams, Raymond. *Television: Technology and Cultural Form.* 3rd ed. London: Routledge Classics, 2003.

Wu, Tim. "Netflix's War on Mass Culture." *New Republic*, 4 December 2013. https://newrepublic.com/article/115687/netflixs-war-mass-culture.

107